SHE *Smiles* AT THE DAYS TO COME

SHE *Smiles* AT THE DAYS TO COME

Rediscovering Beauty, Value, and Hope After Abortion

DIANE PYLE

Scripture quotations taken from the (NASB®) New American Standard Bible®, Copyright © 1960, 1971, 1977, 1995, 2020 by The Lockman Foundation. Used by permission. All rights reserved. lockman.org. Scripture quotations marked (NIV) are taken from the Holy Bible, New International Version®, NIV®. Copyright © 1973, 1978, 1984, 2011 by Biblica, Inc.™ Used by permission of Zondervan. All rights reserved worldwide. Scripture quotations marked (NLT) are taken from the *Holy Bible*, New Living Translation, copyright ©1996, 2004, 2015 by Tyndale House Foundation. Scripture quotations marked MSG are taken from *The Message*, copyright © 1993, 2002, 2018 by Eugene H. Peterson. Used by permission of NavPress. All rights reserved. Represented by Tyndale House Publishers. Scripture quotations marked (ESV) are from The ESV® Bible (The Holy Bible, English Standard Version®), © 2001 by Crossway, a publishing ministry of Good News Publishers. Used by permission. All rights reserved. Scriptures taken from The Voice™. Copyright © 2012 by Ecclesia Bible Society. Used by permission. All rights reserved. Scripture quotations marked TPT are from The Passion Translation®. Copyright © 2017, 2018, 2020 by Passion & Fire Ministries, Inc. Used by permission. All rights reserved. ThePassionTranslation.com.

ISBN Paperback: 978-1-966462-16-3

ISBN Hardback: 978-1-966462-17-0

ISBN Ebook: 978-1-966462-67-5

Library of Congress Control Number: 2025910500

Messenger Books
30 N. Gould Ste. R
Sheridan, WY 82801

Diane Pyle's *She Smiles at the Days to Come* is an essential resource for any woman navigating the complex emotions and unseen wounds after abortion. With compassion and genuine understanding, Diane gently guides readers on a journey of rediscovery—uncovering the beauty, inherent value, and enduring hope that are available through Christ. This book offers a glimpse into the power of grace for individual women, support groups, and anyone seeking to minister to those who suffer. Highly recommended for its honesty, sensitivity, and powerful message of redemption.

—Patricia King
Media Host, Author, and Minister

After twenty-six years of seeking to help women who have experienced abortion, it is safe to say that I have read just about every book published on the subject. *She Smiles at the Days to Come* is unlike any other book on this subject, as the author wisely helps the reader put her reproductive loss in the context of her life experiences. Diane shows the reader how to connect the dots of decisions, misconceptions, trauma, and hurt to better understand why we (who have had abortions) made the choices we did. But best of all, she shares how all the dots can become a tapestry of grace when we surrender it all to our Creator. Diane draws brilliant word pictures that help you embrace both her story and yours. A great read and well worth your time."

—Georgette Forney
Co-founder, Silent No More Awareness Campaign

In *She Smiles at the Days to Come*, Diane Pyle compassionately addresses a topic often shrouded in silence. With gentleness, hope, and strength, she reminds us that even after deep loss, restoration is possible. Through each page, we are invited on a journey of transformation, guided by someone who understands the complexities of grief and the power of faith. This book is a must-read for those longing for healing, who are ready to face the past with grace and the future with a renewed sense of hope and, yes, a smile!

—Teresa Yancy
Author, *Unveiled by God*
Founder, Unlocking Your Book

Diane Pyle is a woman of excellence who has done the hard work and intense research necessary to produce a book that offers her readers and her audiences sound truths and godly wisdom. Like a warm, comforting friend gently taking us by the hand, Diane guides us through her own heart-wrenching journey from trauma to healing. With remarkable transparency, she reveals her healing process so we can follow her path through the shadows of our own traumatic experiences and find beauty, value, and hope in the days to come.

—LaTan Roland Murphy
latanmurphy.com
Award Winning Author

Contents

To the mothers I know and don't know, who, in the face of fear or an uncertain future, took the more difficult road and gave life to your children. You are champions. Your courage inspires me.

A Reflection

To laugh often and much;
to win the respect of the intelligent people
and the affection of children;
to earn the appreciation of honest critics
and endure the betrayal of false friends;
to appreciate beauty;
to find the best in others;
to leave the world a bit better
whether by a healthy child, a garden patch,
or a redeemed social condition;
to know that one life has breathed easier
because you lived here.
This is to have succeeded.
—Ralph Waldo Emerson—

Before We Begin

For years, I heard whispers of encouragement from the books nestled on the shelves of my personal library. They called to me—the roughed-up paperbacks with dog-eared corners and the neatly stacked hardcovers flagged with colorful post-its and scribbled margins—and they waited patiently.

"Stories build confidence and inspire people to dream bigger," said one.[1]

Another declared, "You have something to say. ... Talk to my friends. ... Listen carefully to what you hear. You will discover a cry welling up from the depths of the human heart that has remained unheard because there was no one to listen."[2]

"Lift others from the sorrow of shame to the joy of hope," insisted another.[3]

Atticus Finch, the lawyer from *To Kill A Mockingbird*, fueled the fire when he said, "You never really understand a person until you consider things from his point of view—until you climb into his skin and walk around in it."[4] Through his words, I heard, "They'll never really understand a woman who has had an abortion until they consider things from her point of view—until they climb into her skin and walk around in it."

Then came the challenge: "There can never really be any peace and joy for you until there is peace and joy for them, too."[5]

Suffice it to say these messages, and hundreds more like them, were like seeds sown by a gardener expecting a harvest. They beckoned me to an adventure I didn't feel adequately equipped for. Year by year and day by day, the invitation was ever unfolding.

Two timely encounters—a movie about a World War II battle in Okinawa and conversations with women in Nepal—changed the trajectory of my life and hurled me from the flow of ordinary, anonymous living. There was no mistaking I was being called to write the book you now hold in your hands.

Writing about almost anything else would have been my happy preference. The task of addressing anyone whose memories of her past contain the pain of abortion is daunting. It's a complex topic that continually faces habitual resistance. Because it is often framed as a simple healthcare intervention, some people don't blink an eye when hearing there have been over sixty-three million reported abortions in the last fifty years in the U.S. alone and seventy-three million worldwide each year. And yet, it remains a disturbing and overwhelming topic for many—especially for a woman who's been leveled by accusations and judgments. When telling her story, it's highly likely she purposely omits her abortion experience.

Here's the crucial point. The numbers are staggering. The data is important. However, the danger with numbers and charts is that they are abstract. Mothers with empty arms are not numbers or statistics. Neither are they bare abstractions. They're humans. They don't have the shoulders for the heavy burden they carry. They need to know there's a future beyond their heartache.

I began to wonder about these hurting women. Where are they? Who are they? Where is their voice? How are they managing their conscience, their emotions, their lives? Who do they talk to? Does anyone see their true dignity and worth? It's easy to ignore them because we think we can't help or because we choose not to see them. However, I believe reaching these women is the need of the hour.

When I learned the human mind doesn't handle enormous,

shocking numbers and abstraction very well—our reaction is benumbed indifference—it was an aha moment for me. I understood the importance of moving away from numerical data and establishing some grounds for understanding. I knew that if there was any hope of humanizing the issue—putting a face on the faceless and giving a voice to the voiceless millions of women—then sharing my personal story would be not only helpful but essential.

Time is of the essence to report honestly about this topic. How do I know? When nudged to tell friends and total strangers that my heart had been kindled with a passion to write a message of hope, many responded, with tears welling in their eyes, saying they wished there had been a similar book to read on their journeys to freedom. Women (and men) who managed to escape the life-altering event also confirmed that both a voice and a story are indispensable.

It's my great privilege to let go and risk myself on untried wings to speak to women who are bound by the *unfreedom* that abortion unleashed in their lives. I'm putting the vulnerable, broken places of my humanity in the spotlight so the light of love can shine through. I'm giving my name and telling my story to add soul to you and your story and to each of the millions of women who are still hiding without hope and without light in the shadows of doubts, grief, guilt, and shame.

I'm giving a voice to you if you continue to travail, silently and subconsciously, in the aftermath of abortion. You have been deprived of empathy, compassion, and understanding. You need to know that your foremost needs—forgiveness and true freedom—are in your future.

The tender whisper of Frederick Buechner says it best, "To lend each other a hand when we're falling, perhaps that's the only work that matters in the end."[6] My hope is that I might earn your trust and help open you to ideas you've never before considered. Thank you, beautiful you, for allowing me to quietly bear witness to your beautiful life. I look forward to the journey together.

ONE

For the Sake of One

> *To each there comes in their lifetime*
> *a special moment when they are figuratively*
> *tapped on the shoulder and offered*
> *the chance to do a very special thing,*
> *unique to them and fitted to their talents.*
> *What a tragedy if that moment finds them*
> *unprepared or unqualified for that which*
> *could have been their finest hour.*
> —Winston Churchill—

I VOWED NEVER TO WATCH A WAR MOVIE. THE SIGHT AND SOUND OF helicopters caused my insides to quiver. I had had my fill of military conflict and hostility as a child. But one night, thanks to years of freedom from painful memories and reactions, I agreed to watch Mel Gibson's *Hacksaw Ridge*.[1]

The film contains a tense scene where Pfc. Desmond T. Doss faces a court-martial for disobeying direct orders from commanding officers. Misjudged as a coward and ridiculed for refusing to carry a weapon, he addresses the presiding judge and fervently explains his desire to serve in an Army combat unit: "I need to serve. I have the energy and passion to serve as a medic. Right in the middle with the other guys. No less danger. Just while everybody else is taking life, I'm gonna be saving it. With the world so set on tearing itself apart, doesn't seem like such a bad thing to me to want to put a little bit of it back together."[2]

The judge honors his rights as a conscientious objector, charges are withdrawn, and the case is dismissed. Desmond is ordered to resume his duties and training as a combat medic.

Once derided for his faith and bullied for his refusal to bear arms, Private Doss and the words he spoke before the military court prove true. Final, climactic, and awe-inspiring scenes spotlight the real man and Army hero in the hellfire of battle. After his platoon is met by horrific, violent resistance from the enemy, he ignores orders to retreat from the scene of casualties and single-handedly rescues wounded comrades from the battlefield on Okinawa.

In the face of gunfire and heavy mortar, the Virginia native searches, one by one, for those facing certain death or capture. He drags or carries them, inch by inch, to the edge of the ridge. Using an improvised sling and rope system, he then lowers each man from the escarpment down the jagged, 400-foot vertical cliff into the care and safety of the battalion. Day becomes night. The grueling mission continues. Uninterrupted. He knows minutes can be a matter of life and death. While crawling through hell on earth and among bodies, feeling each for a pulse, he startles a confused and terrified soldier who begins shooting randomly into the dark of night. Desmond springs toward him, covers the soldier's mouth, and whispers, "Pinnick. Pinnick. Pinnick, it's Doss. It's Doss. Be quiet. Just be quiet. I got you."

"I can't see," the soldier replies.

With quiet assurance, Desmond tells him to hold tight as he pours water from a canteen over his eyes. He tenderly dabs them with a cloth. "Try now."

Pinnick opens his eyes and exclaims in great surprise, "I thought I was blind." The pair rejoices. Quietly and briefly. Pinnick's rescue begins.

Throughout the night, Desmond continues to treat and pick up the wounded to bring them to safety. He prays aloud, "Please, Lord, help me get one more. Help me get one more."[3]

A man for the hour, Desmond's mental toughness and physical strength were outmatched only by the strength of his inner man. It's what moved him to serve his country in the cause of freedom in the Second World War. It's what anchored him to stay behind enemy lines after his company had been repulsed with heavy losses. Surrounded by enemy soldiers, he chose not to turn his back on the plague of despair and oppression but to inject himself into the suffering of his fellow man. To be a vessel for what seemed impossible. To run to evacuate the wounded and rescue roughly seventy-five men from the clutches of death.

He never dreamed the call on his life would come in the theater of war. Much less that he would answer it in the aftermath of a 1945 Okinawa bloodbath in desperately dangerous conditions and at grave personal risk. But every day of his life, including his family history and the conflicts and obstacles he faced, was used as training to mold and prepare him, shaping his character and uniquely qualifying him for the precise moment that marked him as a bold, fearless, and influential leader.

As you consider your life after your abortion experience—whether months, years, or decades ago—do you find that you, like Desmond, have faced seasons of feeling misjudged, ridiculed, or misunderstood? Have you suffered through waves of regret, sadness, and "what-ifs?" What about sorrow, grief, shame, or anger? Have you encountered flashbacks or strange dreams? Irritability or even severe distress at the thought of your secret of secrets resurfacing? The aftermath of abortion manifests differently for every woman. It infinitely varies, but it's always filled with difficulties.

Maybe you've adjusted to the more common effects but face recurring emotional strain and physical distress. Maybe you're reaching for personal clarity and heartfelt purpose in your life but feel stuck or held back by an invisible wall of uncertainty. Maybe true happiness, genuine enthusiasm, or a shot at what energizes you and fuels your passion appear to be elusive. Like Desmond, you need a breakthrough.

In my research on abortion and its aftermath, I've become increasingly dismayed about something that's more obvious to me than ever before—millions and millions of us are not as healthy and whole as we think we are. A growing mountain of evidence reveals we're unconsciously trudging in despair. We're plagued by a low-grade hopelessness. A powerful psychological censorship mounts guard over our secrets to keep us silent. We've been ignored and neglected—victims twice over. These truths gain greater clarity with every woman who unlocks her closet of secrets or questions the procedure that was supposed to be safe and uncomplicated. Broken silence and details of our discontent point to a multi-dimensional struggle that cannot be ignored.

What might happen if we were to uncover and trumpet the counternarratives, the disturbing and true stories of each of these millions of women? What might happen if you were to bring the reality of your abortion into your consciousness so you can be free of its intrusions and eruptions in your daily life?

Friend, if the analogy of war ties you in knots or feels heavy, please understand my use of it is purposeful. If you've been through the hellfire of abortion, if it remains buried in secrecy, or if it still bothers you, then you need to know there *is* a war going on. However, there's good news. It's entirely possible to put this profound event into its proper place in the overall arc of your life. There's never been a better time to let down your drawbridge and walk out of your fortress.

Real-life heroes and heroines fascinate me. I'm drawn to the stories of ordinary men and women who have looked at the landscape of the human condition and accepted the burden of running to what has been made clear. Who isn't inspired by unlikely champions on the pages of history who resist complacency, ignore the temptation to twiddle their thumbs, and step into the unknown? Who isn't motivated by those who sacrifice comfort, popularity, safety, the future—their very lives—to reach for what seems impossible?

I'm moved by lionhearted warriors who, despite scoffers and the high pitch of well-intentioned dissuasion, wear trust as a constant companion—not a blind trust but a secure one. Aware of opposition and its accompanying hostility, they march toward the goal at any cost and by any road with no assurance of the outcome. They believe if one person—just *one* person—responds to an outstretched hand and welcomes relief, all of heaven will rejoice. And every minute and all effort expended will have been worth it.

Englishman William Wilberforce, a name too few know, stepped into the arena shortly after his election to Parliament. His motivation? The desire to speak for those who could not. Strengthened and inspired by friends like John Newton (lyricist of *Amazing Grace*), he galvanized a handful of like-minded confidants in 1787 and led a world-changing campaign: the abolition of England's profitable and economically important slave trade. For twenty long years, he spent himself in a worthy cause. Against all odds—the full force of Parliament, an apathetic and decadent citizenry, and threats of Britain's financial disaster—victory came at last. With his small band of brothers and sisters, he brought an end to the slave trade in 1807.

Harriet Tubman, born into slavery on the Eastern Shore of Maryland in 1822, endured the first third of her life as someone else's "property." But no oppression could keep her down. Driven by the innate longing for personal liberty, she escaped to freedom at age twenty-seven. It wasn't long before her heart burned and impelled her to act on behalf of family members and others still chained in physical and emotional bondage.[4] She personally assisted seventy-five or more slaves, including most of her family, as they ran from forced servitude into their personal promised land. Today, among the legendary exploits that earned her titles of "Moses the Deliverer" and "The Moses of Her People," she is best recognized as one of the most famous "conductors" of the Underground Railroad.

Like a true prize fighter, Harriet Beecher Stowe put on her proverbial boxing gloves and stepped into the ring of the most divisive issue of her time. Her goal was not to extract a profit but to advance the idea of the humanity of slaves. One white woman, compelled by strong anti-slavery sentiments, aimed to awaken the conscience of America. She creatively penned her grievances in *Uncle Tom's Cabin* and delivered a knockout. First published in 1852, her masterpiece helped expose the evils of slavery and solidify the anti-war sentiments of the North. It remains a moving, powerful work of literature today.

Golden threads unite this small sample of visionaries. Readied with strength of character, conviction, and compassion, they were driven to rescue strangers and release them from danger, pain, and hardship. Having experienced or witnessed unnecessary suffering and oppression, they committed themselves to the divine relay. To usher those in bondage from the iron-smelting furnace—whether or not the captives perceived their distinct, unique value or anticipated the freedom being won on their behalf.

When called into action, these men and women trusted they were entering their finest hour. Set apart and ignited by an unwavering hope that *all* things can be turned and used for good and for the benefit of others, each became a brilliant flame that could not be ignored.

As I watched *Hacksaw Ridge,* mesmerized by Desmond's unbound grit and ingenuity, a contagious resolve began to build inside me. Walls of paralyzing fear that had hemmed me in began to fall. The vice of my unbending self-preservation loosened its grip.

During the pivotal scene where he awakens to his purpose and turns his gaze to the fighting grounds—toward the men and their cries for help—I, too, was stopped in my tracks. Tears rolled down my cheeks. In an instant, it became clear that what was true for Desmond was equally true for me. Every mile had mattered. Every event of my life including the trials and temptations—good, bad, or indifferent— was at a point of convergence. It was time to abandon the worry of exposure and all my accompanying "what ifs."

At this significant moment, I received the following vision:

Standing at the perimeter of something comparably formidable, I was offered a choice similar to the one presented to Desmond —to turn back or run to. Recognizing either option would become the burden of my future, I saw myself running toward the voices, cries, and silent suffering on what I call the modern-day battlefield.

Though exponentially larger but less visible, this war zone is strikingly similar to the one in which Desmond gave his all. It's littered with heartbreak and ruin. Like Desmond's platoon buddy, Pinnick, the wounded are temporarily blinded. They just don't realize it. They do not recognize these dark grounds. The felt presence of armed soldiers on both sides reminds them to remain silent. One camp aggressively and ruthlessly defends its turf no matter the cost. The other unit retreats into ambivalence, apathy, and disregard for anyone fallen in combat. Both groups are prone to open fire on the wounded and shoot anyone who manages to escape.

No matter the vantage point, it's difficult to discern between those who volunteered to be here and those who were coerced. There are multiple casualties. Untold millions, in fact. All taken in by an elaborate fiction. All scattered in enemy territory. The sound of a faint dirge rises.

It's eerily quiet and intimidating and filled with people like you, people like me. Make no mistake, this is, hands down, the most diverse combat zone in the history of humankind. Women from impoverished families. Women from privilege. Some from the depths of depravity. Some from the best of humanity. The obscure. The famous. The wise. The foolish. The ordinary. The elite. The discarded. The high achieving. The addict. The clean. The uneducated. The enlightened. Paupers. Royalty. Women from every nation, color, language, and generation. The good-

hearted. The heartless. From every religion. The God-loving and the godless.

For many, this unexpected battleground is a first-time experience. It may be their only. For others—veterans—it's strangely familiar territory. An unfortunate rerun. The majority suffer in silence. Isolated. The spark in their eyes is dulled. They drink bitter tears. A handful, triggered by fear, resentment, and anger, shoot aimlessly into the night, projecting their pain on anyone else who tries to hurt them. There is little to no conversation. After all, no one ever truly wanted to be here.

Sorrows, heartbreak, and injuries, those not resulting in death, are as numerous and unique as the number of wounded. Most wounds will fade—at least superficially—and go undetected. For a while anyway. The worst will bring permanent impairment and future loss. Some degree of emotional trauma is a guarantee.

Many seem lifeless. Befooled and degraded. Overcome with hopelessness and despair. Plenty more are scarcely breathing, buried in shame and uncertainty. Some are whimpering, barely holding on. Some nurse a hushed grief, searching for a place to hide. Others lie awake, determined to push through regret with sheer willpower. Pretending.

There is no easy way out. Forever etched into their collective memory is the moment they were wounded in the war. Mocked and tormented in their night hour, they make inner vows to conceal their pain. They rehearse the questions that churn inside their minds: What happened? What have I done? How will I move on? Who will find out?

Nobody escapes the voice of accusation and condemnation. Each woman knows intuitively that "normal" is in the rearview mirror. One thing is certain: No one on this battlefield could have imagined or foreseen the horror, much less that anything good could come out of the dark and harrowing ordeal.

And we wonder if anyone like a Desmond Doss will rise up to pray for "one more." To run into the battle fray. To sweep in to say, "I've got you." To pick up and bring relief to those who feel unworthy. To rescue the mothers with empty arms. To secure the release of every woman who quietly determined her unborn child should die.

I emerged from the vision fully persuaded that I had received a figurative tap on the shoulder. I rehearsed Toni Morrison's instruction again and again: "The function of freedom is to free someone else. If you are no longer wracked or in bondage to a person or a way of life, tell your story. Risk freeing someone else."[5]

I knew it was time to write a trustworthy and genuine message of freedom and healing. A message emptied of messy, false assumptions. A message, to borrow Dr. Mariam Grossman's words, stripped of rigid, polarizing political opinions and ideology and free of self-righteous, accusatory finger-pointing.[6] A bold message of hope devoid of ear-piercing, unbending claims of "Abortion is a right," and "Abortion is mercy," and wholesale, insensitive rants like, "God's judging the nation because of abortion."

Error and condemnation backfire every time. Bombastic, strident comments, even if they're not aimed at us women who have been flattened by abortion, only make matters worse. Incivility grinds us more inward, keeping us in hiding and causing us to reject the very help we need. Women who are sunk in sorrow and desperate to breathe again need truth framed in comforting, loving words—words that effectively communicate somebody's rooting for us and working for our well-being.

If we women on the battlefield are ever going to get home, we must resist the dramatic plea to pay no attention to the man behind the curtain. We must bust his buttons and peer behind all the veils and screens and neatly crafted jargon and slogans. We must pay attention to what's actually there. It's imperative that we shift to meaningful, edifying conversations about the many facets of abortion and declare there's hope beyond its heart-rending memories. It's time to take the guesswork out of the issue and lovingly provide answers so the needs of every post-abortion woman can surface and be acknowledged.

Here's the crux of the matter: In spite of all the preconceived beliefs and cognitive biases, abortion is *not* a political issue. At the highest heights and deepest depths, it's a matter of life and death. So it's truly a *human* issue. To fall is human. To fail is human. To miss the mark is human.

It's important to assert—this cannot be understated—that for far too long, the culture, organizations, and institutions, both religious and secular alike, have wrongly placed abortion and its aftereffects beyond the scope of human experience. It's been championed as something so "safe and effective" that it couldn't possibly bring heartache. It's also been treated as something so prickly and inflammatory that it mustn't be touched—like leprosy that should be avoided at all costs or kept behind closed doors. It has been stamped as an act far outside the possibility of being forgiven. The devastating and dire result? Millions of us women are hobbling and limping along, at least subconsciously, utterly convinced that all is quiet and calm. Or we're fully persuaded we're failures who can never have a happy ending.

An honest look reveals that abortion is like all the other universal concerns and dysfunctions that affect humankind. Lisa Rowe, a psychotherapist committed to providing support, help, and healing after abortion, emphasizes it's hard for anyone to get through life without experiencing some form of trauma. She describes abortion as just *one* event in the family of adverse human events. She highlights research that shows one in four women will experience abortion before her forty-fifth birthday and reminds us we're only two people removed from someone who has had an abortion. I've heard her say abortion is not unlike any other unfavorable event that humanity experiences as we try to manage our lives in light of all the traumas and wounds that unfold in our world, such as infidelity, divorce, substance abuse, physical abuse, anxiety, depression, self-harm, and eating disorders. We can believe a voice like hers because, trust me, she speaks with a love accent.[7]

So breathe easy. Rest assured. I'm declaring this a neutral zone. The spirit of my message has *nothing* to do with the current cultural debate—whether it's moral or political. Right or wrong. Whether it should be approached from the ideological left or the ideological right. Or whether it should be legislated or adjudicated. All of these are important subjects, but these discussions are better left to the advocates and combatants on both sides.

My focus is not on abortion. My emphasis is on you, the mother.

My goal is to speak tenderly from my heart to your heart and from my true self to your true self. I aim to address the matter as openly as any other hidden anguish and remorse we face in life. I hope to create an atmosphere in which you're free to confront your secret and gain victory over it. Indeed, the message is not for the battlefield at large but for the woman who's caught in the crosshairs of this deeply polarized issue and feels stuck in between. For the one who senses and is receptive to the winds of change. For the one who yearns to escape the chasm of despair and mend the rift. For the one who's tired of running away. For the one who desires to tear off the seal of secrecy and cast off the guilt, stigma, and shame of the battlefield. My message is for the woman who's ready to reclaim her freedom and cling to hope.

Could it be that you are one of these tender, beloved women? If so, you might be asking yourself why you should listen to me. It's a brilliant question. Why me? Precisely because I've been there.

The old saying rings true: It takes one to know one. To use Brennan Manning's analogy, I'm that converted, persuasive travel agent handing out brochures to a place I've visited.[8] Once hindered by deep-rooted shame and a false belief that my faults and imperfections and history of abortion disqualified me from addressing the issue with others, I put myself on a shelf. It was much easier to masquerade as though I had never faced this kind of earth-shattering, tectonic-plate-shifting trauma.

I couldn't have been more wrong.

Fellow traveler, I believe my experience renders me fully qualified to journey with you. Conversations I've had in recent years with other women who have been set free from their past validate the claim. I now embrace the importance of disclosing to you something of my vulnerable side—my dark place—and resisting the temptation to convey a perfect image. "Projecting the flawless image keeps us from reaching people who feel we just wouldn't understand them."[9] I'm willing to take the risk of divulging my story because I'm confident, as Anne Lamotte asserts, that shining the light on the dark exposes not our baseness but our humanity.[10] All of us on this spinning orb have gone astray and need refreshing.

I don't pretend or presume to be some superhero sweeping in to "save the day." The war is far too old, too long, and too wide for any one person to conquer. Its roots extend to the dawn of civilization. I am convinced, though, that to remain unmoved and uninvolved is cowardly. I can no longer, in good conscience, park on the sidelines as the entrenched armies on both sides of the issue continue to fortify and advocate for their positions while hurling pitchforks of contempt and shooting arrows of judgment at those of us trapped in the gorge that divides them. Time is short. The stakes are high.

I understand it's easy to distance ourselves from those we can't help—or from those we *think* we can't help. However, avoiding the issue because it touches on sore spots or refusing to address it because it's unpleasant does more harm than good. Furthermore, ignoring the millions of injured, weary souls lingering on the battlefield is cruel. They already carry a heavy load of feeling forsaken and too far gone. They need somebody to eagerly champion their cause and proclaim good in their future.

"Where there is breath," says a dear friend of mine, "there is hope."

I'm reminded of the scene in *Toy Story* when a soldier gets side-swiped and crushed.[11] His sergeant runs to the scene of the casualty and ignores the wounded man's half-hearted cry of "Go on without me! Just go!" He swiftly pulls him to safety, and, in a display of strength and loyalty, insists, "A good soldier never leaves a man behind."[12]

In *The Wisdom of Tenderness,* Brennan Manning explains that people who have experiential knowledge of a particular pain have a deeper degree of compassion for others with the same pain. He conveys the truth that our wounds empower us to heal others: "Grace and healing are communicated through the vulnerability of men and women who have been broken on the wheels of living. … In Love's service only wounded soldiers can serve.'"[13]

So here I am. And, friend, here you are. We have been to hell and back with the battle scars to show for it. I'm a woman, a wife, a mother, a daughter, a sister, a niece, an aunt, a cousin, and a friend who is willing to convey, with wholehearted empathy, that I *do* understand. My first-hand experience compels me and fuels my determination to act, to share my story and declare to you that you are worthy of true peace, deep love, and freedom from old guilts and enslaved thought patterns, and to point you to the way off this invisible battlefield so you can truly start living.

Members of Alcoholics Anonymous say that to free the captive, one must name the captivity. They know we can't leave a captivity we cannot see. Too many of us who have experienced abortion have erected protective structures to hide our wounds. We have avoided dealing with them, and we've become comfortable with our unhealthy responses and habits. Concealing and denying these hurts has led us to living the illusion of a life of freedom.

The reality is we have been drawn into crippling silence and chained to the emotional, physical, and spiritual consequences of having taken the lives of our unborn children. We walk on wobbly knees. Whether seven days ago, seven months ago, or seven decades ago, we never forget that choice. And too few have any idea that when we choose honesty about the event, stop hiding, and courageously face it, good news awaits us.

No doubt, this is a messy, complicated issue. Contentious. Toe-curling. Grotesque. Difficult if not hellish. A lodestone that can simultaneously draw absolute silence and ignite explosive opinions. It makes everybody feel uncomfortable. I'm convinced, however, that like water to a thirsty soul, you are the woman who sits in this parched land, longing for a spring that flows with refreshment and restoration. Will you welcome a release from captivity—something that perhaps you never imagined nor dreamed possible? Might you consider an invitation to take the necessary steps forward toward discovering your true self?

Your rescue is long overdue. For the sake of one, my aim is to reach you, to say, "I've got you!" and to strengthen you so you can run.

A REFLECTION

Perhaps you have become so comfortable with the wounds of your choice that you don't recognize the invisible chains that keep you from living your best life. It's equally possible you've resigned yourself to the belief that you deserve these wounds and shackles. More than likely, it probably never entered your mind to confront your choice and lay aside every weight and hindrance associated with it. Might you consider that owning your story can be hard but not nearly as difficult as spending your life running from it? Friend, you had a choice that day. And you have a choice today. I encourage you to join me in choosing the path to freedom.

P.S. You are loved.

TWO

No Stranger to War

You can't connect the dots looking forward.
You can only connect them looking backward.
—Steve Jobs—

W RITER AND HUMORIST S YDNEY S MITH IS CREDITED WITH SAYING, "Ah, you flavor everything; you are the vanilla of society."[1] From the lips of a kindhearted person, the quip is likely intended as a sweet compliment. From the tongue of a sharp-witted person, it might be a slyly delivered insult. After all, if you've ever tried vanilla extract by itself, you know the flavoring is complex and bitter. It's mystifying that a taste so highly unpleasant, surprisingly unsavory, and so foul-tasting can enhance the flavor of and give depth to an entire recipe.

If we're being perfectly honest, each of us can admit to having an unpleasant or unsavory ingredient in her life. For many of us with experience on the battlefield, it's obvious and easily identifiable. My goodness, we've crawled for inches and miles on the road of shaken assurance and crippled confidence. We've run for days and years trying to escape the memory of the day we were wounded in the war. We've become weary trying to dodge the arrows of our past. Given the opportunity, who of us wouldn't hesitate to remove the element that shifted or derailed what might have been our preferable future?

The reality is that it has been hard, if not impossible, to lay aside the guilt and guilt-driven grief. We feel powerless to make a change. We wish hocus-pocus, abracadabra, and bibbidi-bobbidi-boo it could all just go away.

Friend, I'd like to ask you a question. What if the ingredient you'd most like to eliminate can take on meaning to such a degree that, like vanilla, when it's worked into the entire recipe, it can enhance and give depth to your life?

Communication coach and author Carmine Gallo highlights the research of Dr. Richard Tedeschi and Dr. Lawrence Calhoun, psychology professors and researchers at the University of North Carolina, Charlotte. They are pioneers in the field of "Posttraumatic Growth," the process that people go through in the aftermath of adverse and traumatic life events. Their studies illuminate how tragedy, suffering, and loss can be turned to our advantage—much like the crushing and pressing that brings forth diamonds and pearls. We can emerge from struggle and tension with newfound strength, meaning, and a renewed sense of purpose in our lives *because* of a traumatic event. Gallo describes their posttraumatic growth model this way:

> A person experiences a "seismic event" that disrupts their internal narrative, the story they expected their life to take. The event leads to "rumination," where they turn things over in their minds to make sense of the event. Rumination is followed by "self-disclosure," where they become comfortable writing and talking about the event. They are eager to share how the event changed them for the better.[2]

I'd like to introduce you to two historically famous people. Their individual backstories make any rational person wince, and yet their life narratives attest to the belief that we can make peace with our past and press on to be world changers. No matter who we are, where we've been, or what we've done, trauma can be transformed.

Englishman John Newton joined the ranks as a sailor in the transatlantic slave trade during his late teens. He later captained voyages trafficking African slaves to the West Indies. Poor health forced him to return to his mother country to find new work. When he came to his senses, he admitted to himself that he struggled with and despised his role in transporting slaves. In a remarkable turn, in the better part of his life, he used his background as a slave trader to speak and argue against his former occupation.

Memories of what he witnessed during years of barbarous cruelty and inhumane treatment of the slaves fueled his new passion and purpose: a decades-long endeavor to abolish the slave trade. Driven by the conviction that his silence would be criminal, "the competent witness" (as Newton called himself) chose to expose the horrors of what he had seen and heard.[3] He detailed his personal involvement in "that unhappy and disgraceful branch of commerce" in *Thoughts Upon The African Slave Trade*.[4] The pamphlet, which also served as a public confession, was published and sold for one shilling. He also mentored William Wilberforce in his parliamentary effort to end the deadly practice. Perhaps his greatest legacy came in writing the lyrics to the world-renowned song of redemption and hope, "Amazing Grace."

King David, Michelangelo's famous, towering, seventeen-feet-tall marble sculpture I saw in Florence's Accademia Gallery, was nothing more to me than a name, a statue, and an object to observe. More than a decade passed before I took an interest in the real life of this legendary king—the historical man, not the physically superior, fabricated, sculpted version.

David's backstory reads like one many of us can relate to. It has all the raw and real-world elements of a life common to the everyday man or woman. He wasn't spared the day-to-day struggles, tension, and pain. He had no mother to raise him. The youngest in his family, he was mocked and treated as the least favorite. He was a fighter and an underdog. For no sensible reason, he was envied and despised and had only a few close friends. He endured nearly ten years in the wilderness, running for his life. The detail that grabbed me by the nape of my neck is that as a crowned king, he was personally responsible for taking the life of his lover's husband. Wow! Yet, in spite of this egregious error, he reigned for forty years and is remembered as Israel's greatest king.

When I first read about John Newton and King David, I was genuinely puzzled. It seemed, based on my limited human knowledge, they should have been sidelined or shelved for the rest of time. I needed an explanation of how someone can overcome the shackles of adversity and poor choices. What makes an ordinary man eligible, after trudging through life carrying the weight of failings and fallings, for a life of restored strength, confidence, trustworthiness, and love? How does anyone with questionable character, without the benefit and the promises of twenty-first century "reputation management," rise from the ashes to become a masterpiece?

Frederick Buechner inspires and gently entreats us to consider a heartening and fortifying point of reflection:

> The sad things that happened long ago will always remain part of who we are just as the glad and gracious things will too, but instead of being a burden of guilt, recrimination, and regret that make us constantly stumble as we go, even the saddest things can become, once we have made peace with them, a source of wisdom and strength for the journey that still lies ahead. It is through memory that we are able to reclaim much of our lives that we have long since written off by finding that in everything that has happened to us over the years … we are offered possibilities of new life and healing which, though we may have missed them at the time, we can still choose and be brought to life by and healed by all these years later.[5]

There is a flicker of hope. Elsewhere Buechner writes,

> "It's hard to share not just the shallows of your life, which is what we're all so good at doing, but to speak out of the depths of your life—the depths are scary. To go down into the depths of your past, to go down into the depths of your secrets, to go down to the depths of your

pain is a scary business … You can never be sure you're going to find a pearl in the depths; you find MONSTERS in the depths. But it seems to me that what you do find in the depths is yourself and each other."[6]

The memories. The depths. Pearls. Each other.

Friend, as painful as it is to walk back through doorways we'd rather keep closed and rooms we'd rather keep bolted, there's great potential and value in returning to our formative years. Can we possibly believe, as demonstrated in the lives of John Newton and King David, that all things can somehow be used or woven together for good in our lives? *All* things—the good, the bad, and, yes, the ugly?

As we journey through memories, depths, and secrets, it may help to ask yourself questions like: What if? What if all my struggles, insecurities, and the inner tension that led to and then resulted from the traumatic event in my life could be turned into strength, confident hope, and triumph? What if all the adversity and everything intended to take me out could be turned on its head? What if my stuffed, dry, and broken straw life can be spun into golden threads?

———

I'm no stranger to war. The cosmic battle for my life started the day I was born.

My father, a United States Naval Academy graduate and naval aviator, was halfway around the world. His squadron was attached to the USS *Enterprise*, the aircraft carrier that led the 1964 convoy on an around-the-world cruise. The mission, an extension of an already long, six-month deployment, was named *Operation Sea Orbit*. The carrier group was cutting through global waters as a statement to the world of America's naval power and technical achievement. The fleet was all-nuclear. The first of its kind. All sixty-four days and 30,500 miles of it.

A side note about that sweltering summer day is that while I didn't yet have a name, I was crowned with my first title, "Little Miss Sea Orbit." For as long as I can remember, my father loved to reminisce about the accolade. He beamed with pride whenever he regaled others with his storytelling.

"You won't believe it!" always included other eyebrow raising facts about why he wasn't holding my mom's hand in the delivery room. While it was hot in Mom's hometown, he was engrossed in the razzmatazz of a sizzling, humid seaport of Karachi, Pakistan, on the Arabian Sea. When the telegram announcing my birth arrived, he and his friends were on the streets downtown, spellbound by the Indian cobras dancing and swaying as the snake charmers played their *pungis*. The significance of the connection between Little Miss Sea Orbit and snake charmers would eventually come to light. The most baffling detail for me is that I wasn't given a name until three days after my birth.

No name? I know, it's an oddity in the twenty-first century. Naming a baby today sometime between "We're having a girl" and "Welcome to the world, Hortense!" seems less daunting.

My parents' first pregnancy predated routine ultrasounds. Whether they were having a girl or a boy was a complete mystery, and their concerns were far weightier—before, during, and after my arrival. For starters, they were separated by oceans, seas, and continents. International telephone calls were rare and expensive. Between January and August, they exchanged handwritten letters and possible baby names. The letters took seven to ten days to get to and from the ship. More than a dozen yielded no agreement.

It was also a scary time for expectant parents in the United States. A nationwide viral rubella outbreak loomed large. The fear of thousands of miscarriages, congenital malformations of newborns, and deaths of young babies was very real. My mother decided pregnancy would be easier in familiar territory than in the navy town where she had lived for less than a year. So with the help of one of her sisters, she packed up and drove a thousand miles to her hometown for the support and love of her parents, family, and friends.

Sometime in her last trimester, she received a crushing blow: The Navy was extending my father's deployment. His ship would lead *Operation Sea Orbit*. Excitement for his impending return to celebrate all things wife and baby evaporated. He would not be home in time for my entrance into the world.

While I was growing up and trying to understand the events and circumstances related to the day of my birth, my parents happily answered questions. Four Western Union telegrams and the official birth announcement of Little Miss Sea Orbit are proof of their flurried, three-day attempt to reach an agreement for the name of their firstborn. For the record, my mother prevailed in naming me. Nonetheless, a sense of normalcy about my early life remained elusive to me.

Mom and I lived with my grandparents until Dad returned stateside. He saw and held me for the first time when I was almost seven weeks old. We moved to a small beach cottage near the ocean and the air base. A happy life together seemed anything but certain. Military buildup and the intensity of incidents and provocations in Asia were escalating. The nation was fully committed to war in Vietnam.

Five months later, my father was deployed again to the Mediterranean. Following that deployment, we all relocated to the West Coast for a two-year tour with the Air Force and welcomed a baby brother. In brief, life was disjointed until we resettled, within weeks of my fourth birthday, in the sprawling navy town on the East Coast where I lived out the rest of my childhood…in a bubble.

Our home was in a family-centered neighborhood where we kids were free to host lemonade stands and peddle our Big Wheels and tricycles in the cul-de-sac. As we grew, it was equally safe to ride bikes to piano lessons, a friend's house, or to parties. I could easily answer Sesame Street's famous question, "Who are the people in your neighborhood?"

Everyone I knew was Navy and Catholic…or so I thought. Except for a few swim team pals, we were all nestled in homes among the two elementary schools, six churches, and the lone fire station that dotted our "small" neighborhood. I often wondered who attended the five smaller churches that weren't mine. Whenever my family would visit relatives and friends in other towns, I noticed their neighborhoods were arranged in neat squares and outlined in cement sidewalks. How peculiar! Our streets were as windy and curvy as the yellow brick road, and we didn't have sidewalks. Equally strange was an awareness that the fathers in those towns, dressed in suits and ties, never left their families except to commute by car or train to their day jobs. Convinced those dads weren't as brave as mine, it was easier to shrug off my observation.

What made our community truly unique was the large number of active duty and retired military families who called it home. It's no exaggeration that only a sprinkling of civilian neighbors in our little corner of the world helped break up the monotony. Dad's commute to work wasn't far—his office was at a master jet base. Whenever we played outside, we often waved to our fathers and neighbors as they drove to and from work wearing flight suits and uniforms. Any sudden decrease in the number of cars usually meant they had been deployed somewhere in the world for training exercises or active engagement in the war.

It's important to note—especially for the more than 98% of civilians with no ties to the military—that Navy families are a close-knit group. We experienced life and death together for years. Literally. Most can only imagine the deep friendships and tight bonds among those in our neighborhood. Our lives were woven together like a tapestry, especially because of war.

My two younger brothers (the youngest arriving the year I turned nine) and I had the great fortune of a full-time superhero mom whose presence gave us the stability we needed whether our father was home or away. She influenced us with praise and positivity, encouraged us to learn and to have fun, and supported us in our schoolwork, activities, and sports. We were, by all appearances, a quintessential all-American, middle-class family. Schools didn't single out or celebrate "Month of the Military Child" in those days. Being a Navy family was our normal. But the truth is that our upbringing was *anything but* normal.

Because our dad was a combat fighter pilot, we belonged to a notably uncommon and strikingly small slice of the "occupation" pie chart. We experienced, as every family does, seasons that vacillated between idyllic and complex; however, everyday life was more complicated because of the thorny stresses, tensions, and pressures associated with wartime Navy life. They effectively expanded the normal range of adverse experiences for all of us. Sure, we enjoyed unique perks thanks to the Navy, but on a subconscious level, we forfeited and sacrificed a lot.

In all, my father was deployed overseas for a combined ten of the first twenty years of my life. That's half! Many of his deployments lasted weeks or several months. Short, temporary ones were like the hiccups; they rarely phased us. The extended cruises, though, the ones that seemed painfully endless, lasted anywhere from six to ten months. Invariably, something major on the home front would break or fall apart, like an arm bone or the dishwasher. And we kids would have celebrated another birthday, lost teeth or grown new ones, or marked another six inches of growth on the closet door before Dad returned.

In my formative years, I didn't fully understand why he seemed to come and go like the prevailing wind. The "why" behind his prolonged absences—"Daddy's protecting and defending freedom"—gets lost on a little person. And having an unavailable parent hinders the normal development of a child's mind and heart.

Even though departures were familiar—numbingly so—nothing could minimize the sting and stress of saying goodbye. I remember spending hours, if not days, feeling utterly deflated after Dad shipped off. Separation hurt. Even little things like dinners without Dad seated at the head of the table increasingly magnified my sense of emptiness. The only upside to his absence was that Mom didn't demand that we eat foods we didn't particularly care for—like yucky coleslaw.

Eventually, the proverbial breeze would blow again and refill my sail. Like a lifeline, a letter with Dad's neatly written print would arrive from somewhere far across the globe. Each one was a treasure. I'd read and re-read them all. Then somehow I'd manage to get back into the rhythm of my school routine and all things "little girl."

While the weeks and months spent apart were tough, it's equally true that homecomings tied my emotions into knots. Make no mistake: I *always* looked forward to my father's return. Brave and tough Dad on the home front made everything feel orderly, together, safe, and secure. Normal. But every fly-in—the return and welcome of the squadrons after being deployed—was accompanied by a strange tension, a taut and tangled web of excitement, relief, and sorrow.

I distinctly remember the reruns of standing on the tarmac just outside the hangar with my family and other squadron families. Together, hands waving American flags, we watched the fighter jets land and taxi from the runway toward us. Anticipation would trigger tears. They'd trickle down my cheeks while waiting for my dad to park his plane. Joy and pride would burst within us as we watched him exit the cockpit and descend the ladder. He would survey the crowd, lock eyes with us and smile, then stroll our way. After greeting us in his sweaty flight suit—a smell always commingled with his Doublemint chewing gum—he'd extend his arms, gather all of us together, and embrace us with a strong, papa bear hug. Every hug was one for the record books.

Home-at-last reunion hugs effectively validated another safe return and reinforced the feeling that we had missed him and that he had missed all of us. But they never seemed long enough or strong enough to heal the heartache of separation. Or the sadness of time lost.

Despite the love and support of both our extended and Navy families, the number of these internal roller-coaster rides eventually took its toll. The valleys of farewells and peaks of "Dad's back" weirdly increased family tensions, sibling rivalry, and internal strife. The ebb and flow of change was unsettling. Emotional connectedness waned thin, and an ever-so-subtle sense of abandonment and insecurity seemed to increase the older I got.

The government summoned many of our airmen neighbors to battle in Vietnam. As they were called to put their years of training into action, we were all tested, stretched, and tried. My uncle was shot down and miraculously rescued. We lived among neighbors whose husbands and fathers had been shot down and held and tortured as prisoners of war

(POWs). Two were held for seven years. Others were killed or missing in action (MIAs). The families of those who had been shot down endured agonizing separation. We mourned and grieved alongside them.

Just outside the main gate of the naval jet base, a special monument was erected. The Flame of Hope Memorial, a continually burning flame, stands in the center of a small plot of grassy lawn with sparsely planted shade trees. The inscription on its marker reads, "This flame will burn continuously to light the way for the return of our prisoners of war held in South East Asia." The tribute expanded to include aviators missing in action, too. We all wore bracelets engraved with the names of these heroes and the date they went missing or were captured. We tied yellow ribbons around trees in our front yards to proclaim support for our absent fathers, neighbors, and all those who were missing or imprisoned.

I was seven years old when my father's squadron was called to the Vietnam War. Mrs. Dawson was my second-grade teacher. I wore, coincidentally, a navy blue costume—complete with a white sailor's hat—for my spring gymnastics recital. Reminders of separation lurked everywhere. This deployment, from the start, was different. We knew in advance that the mission was not for training but for combat. To say it was a sobering time for our family is an understatement. Fear of danger and the unknown can be crippling. We were gripped by it.

Vietnam was America's first-ever war to be reported on daily television. Evening newscasts of wartime developments flickered in the family room and brought a constant infusion of angst. I think we watched every one. They linger like vivid, flashing neon signs. Broadcasts rarely ended without haunting visual footage of U.S. helicopters and troops in combat. Walter Cronkite's signature sign-off, "And that's the way it is," echoed off the walls of our house and inside my brain. He repeated the phrase night after night. I believed every word, and I internalized it. He may as well have said, "Deal with it."

Each day served up another chilling reminder that danger was real. Our family, each one of us in his or her own way, carried a subconscious burden, a subtle, nagging dread that senior Navy officials might call or visit us to deliver a devastating report. Men in formal military uniform knocking at the door of a home signaled impending news of either an accident, capture, or death.

To our great fortune, my father avoided enemy gunfire and accidents while in Vietnam. He returned home safely to the family who hadn't seen him for over a year. At first glance, this homecoming seemed similar to all the others. Dad, though, had not come home from a typical deployment focused on readiness exercises. He returned from a real-time, unconventional war.

For anyone not personally acquainted with military life, it's important to note that war is a double-edged sword. It's a powerful external event that simultaneously breaks and toughens both those engaged in the fierce fight *and* their families. The Vietnam War was no different. It left no family unscathed, including ours. My dad had seen and had been actively engaged in warfare—something outside the normal range of human experience. This was a wholly different kind of trauma—one more severe than any natural disaster and far beyond anything he shared in common with any of us. Something was very different: He was a changed man, husband, son, and father.

The evidence was both obvious and acute, even to a small girl just eight years old. At first, I observed that my father stopped taking communion on Sundays. Then it wasn't long before he stopped attending church, except for Christmas and Easter. His sunny and playful disposition, the one I so eagerly, if not desperately, tried to anchor at the forefront of my thoughts about him, gave way to a demeanor and moods that weren't volatile—just difficult to read. I wondered what had happened to the daddy who used to hold and protect me when we swam in the big waves. Where was the fun-loving man who used to tickle and throw me like a basketball high into the air and catch me? He certainly didn't laugh as much.

The long and short of it, as I perceived it anyway, is that it didn't take long for him to lose interest in the things that were important to me. While I would have proudly claimed him as my father—at any moment and in front of anyone—I became less enthusiastic about seeking him out to take a bike ride together or to tap into his genius for help with my math homework. I discerned a waning interest in my activities and noticed his limited attendance at my events and games. Sadly, I remember very little engaging, substantive conversation with him after Vietnam.

The most painful part came when he disengaged and became emotionally unavailable. I can't pinpoint the day or the season, but one thing is certain: I felt invisible and didn't have the maturity, the tools, or the drive to stay connected to him. As Frederick Beuchner says, "A child takes life as it comes because he has no other way of taking it."[7]

Soon enough, rejection, a feeling that had lingered like a familiar but increasingly annoying visitor, moved in. And without realizing it, I had unknowingly welcomed its best friends: resentment and bitterness. Like the impact of a small stone on a windshield, the stress and fractures began to work their effects on my mind and in my heart.

While the fractures would continue to lengthen and splinter, I experienced small personal victories at school and in sports. Teachers and coaches provided positive affirmation, and I appreciated it. I never took for granted any of the love I received from my immediate family and our large extended family. They modeled and influenced us with good values, manners, and morals and provided for every material need. I recognized and felt thankful for the goodness that came my way.

However, what I needed most was age-appropriate, open, and honest dialogue and reassurance that no one escapes the rocks that life throws our way. I needed someone to help me process my internal world—my emotions, the self-talk, and all the curiosities. Someone to help me understand the changes in the home where I was growing up and make sense of my external world. I needed to hear that everyone is a work in progress and that even adults limp and hobble along because of their individual issues. It would have been helpful to hear that no family is perfect and that it's perfectly normal for five people of different ages living and doing life together under one roof to have difficulties—including the challenging and messy seasons that result in untidy backstories.

All kids need to know—and we adults need to remember—that the world we live in is neither a sterile nor sanitized place where nothing goes wrong. Struggles are normal. They come and go and have the potential to one day make us stronger, more resilient, flexible, tender-hearted, and even humble. As Eugene Peterson says, "Everyone's childhood serves up the raw material that is shaped by grace into the life of mature faith."[8]

A REFLECTION

In his book, The Storyteller's Secret, *Carmine Gallo recommends paying attention to our past because it holds the stories of where we've been and how we got to where we are. He says the stories of our past can actually help move us forward. We who have experienced pain, struggle, or despair can be empowered by our experience when we've developed the courage to embrace our backstory, learn from our failures, and share our lessons of struggle with others.*[9]

P.S. You are loved.

THREE

The Crowning and the Crisis

Many a man wishes he were strong enough
To tear a telephone book in half—especially
If he has a teenage daughter.
—Guy Lombardo—

SEX EDUCATION WASN'T PART OF THE OFFICIAL CURRICULUM WHEN I was in school. Somehow, it managed to slither in and, despite my aversion to it, settle itself into the recesses of my mind.

I suspect many of us were starved of helpful and meaningful instruction about human intimacy. I didn't grow up in a home where the topic was addressed at the dinner table—or anywhere, for that matter. My middle school health teacher taught a brief unit on drugs and sexually transmitted diseases. She showed graphic pictures to caution us against taking risky chances and to emphasize the dangers and consequences of indulging. Most of us were a little repulsed, if not horrified. My take was that the images were a bit gross and seemingly irrelevant: No young kid sets out to become a druggie or a woman of the streets.

What we lacked was a wholesome approach to the basics. A foundation. We needed someone not to scare us but to help us develop the right sense of direction and confidence to evaluate things as they actually are, not as they appear to be. We needed, as Dr. Henry Cloud describes, "sound guidance from parents and other authority figures that upholds the value of sex and gives proper guidelines and limits without being repressive."[1]

Most of us, no doubt, were left to our own imaginations. We weren't equipped with the tools needed to help us stand firm against the culture or the people who would lead or pressure us one day to give it all away. The teaching in my home was a sincere but meager admonition: "That's for marriage." Nobody told me that promiscuity promises everything that abstinence guarantees.

Oh, how I wish someone would have gifted me with guidance about the what and why and the benefits of something so important. Heartfelt instruction about investing in honor and self-respect over momentary desires and temptations would have served me well. At the very least, it would have been helpful for somebody to tell me I didn't have to be a product of the culture or that waiting for my Prince Charming and awakening to his kiss would yield a greater "happily ever after" than arriving at his front door carrying heavy baggage. As a friend told me recently, "An honest person doesn't say, 'Wow! I'm so glad I didn't wait.'"

When I consider the books in my personal library—the ones I purchased to inform my parenting and help me understand my early and teenage years—it's safe to articulate what I've understood intuitively for decades: the cultural movement to accept, endorse, promote, and normalize sex without boundaries seems purposeful. Indeed, the hippie-inspired decade of "peace-love-dove" and the sex-outside-marriage free-for-all tied to the Vietnam War started as something the size of a capillary wave. It has swelled, though, into today's onslaught of surging and plunging storm waves—if not subterranean tidal waves—with all their attendant risks and hazards, including abortion. One of the biggest unintended consequences of the sexual revolution is that it sucked up and dumped out countless women into the confusion of churning whitewater. It pulled them down and dragged them under, leaving them gasping, wondering if or when they'd ever come up for air.

The first jolt hit me at the outset of fourth grade. It was, coincidentally, the year of the Roe v. Wade ruling. I had just finished playing "Joy to the World" on the piano for a classmate. Not Isaac Watts's 1719 Christmas carol but the popular 1971 song performed by Three Dog Night. I liked the song because the music was peppy, and I found it quite silly that somewhere out in the world there was a bullfrog named Jeremiah. The idea, too, of throwing away the war brought me joy. Two dear family friends who languished for over seven years in the Hanoi Hilton, Vietnam's infamous torture prison, had been released. The war was still not over.

As we sat on the piano bench, Ali, the youngest of four daughters, zeroed in on the sheet music, took a deep breath, and asked, "Do you know what it means in the song when they sing 'make and sweet and love'?"

"No!" I replied innocently.

She looked over her shoulder to make sure the coast was clear then whispered to me her nine-year-old version of the birds and the bees—complete with descriptive sign language. Short and to the point, the revelation was news to my ears and eyes. Ewwww! I had never heard or seen anything like that before. It tied me in a knot. For goodness sake, we had a new baby in our home!

Fast forward a few years. Elementary school was in my rearview mirror. My emotional drawbridge was still up, but now I was trying to swim out of a rip current of low self-esteem. A feeling of being small and less-than, both emotionally and physically, consumed me. I was recovering from nicknames like Little Bit, Knee High, and Peanut and enduring the embarrassment of being a late bloomer.

52 Things Daughters Need From Their Dads was decades away from landing on anyone's bookshelf. For that matter, so were other important books like *Sex Has a Price Tag, Hooked,* and *Unprotected.*

As for me, I was floundering in my attempts to believe I was still worthy of my dad's love or acceptance.

In a mysterious but uplifting twist, during the final weeks of eighth grade, I tried out and made the cheerleading squad and was voted into student government. It felt like I had a fresh lease on life that catapulted me through a new door. Formerly a "commoner," I took my place among the leaders and popular kids in my class and stepped into ninth grade to rule and reign during the final year of middle school.

The school year exceeded my expectations. Cheering, sports, clubs, and school dances were highlights. And so was the long-anticipated, big-deal retreat with my Catholic friends for Confirmation. Billed as a time of final preparation before taking the mature step to affirm and strengthen one's faith, the two-day period of seclusion and solitude for me was quite remarkable. But not in the way you might think. The retreat is forever etched in my memory as one complete and unholy disaster. A set-up of epic proportions. I remember nothing more than another peer-led, shocking teaching on sex.

Before I tell you about that weekend, I need to describe an unusual experience from several weeks prior. One afternoon, my aunt, uncle (the one who was shot down and rescued in a Vietnam jungle), and four cousins (the ones I played dress-up with at our grandparents' house every summer) visited our home. From the living room, I watched my father greet them in the foyer. He welcomed each one with big smiles, compliments, and hugs like he used to give me. It seemed more like a spontaneous celebration than a typical family visit—like they had walked in with the elusive bullfrog Jeremiah. I longed to share that kind of cheerfulness with Dad again. Just like the good ole days.

As I observed the exchange of pleasantries and listened to their chitter-chatter, a harsh voice rudely barged in. *Look at that. He doesn't love you like he loves them.* The poison arrow of negative thoughts effectively and precisely hit its bull's-eye. A rush of sadness flooded my heart. Anger and pain followed close behind. It took everything in me to resist the urge to shout, *I'm your daughter, for crying out loud!*

Deep down, my soul begged, *Don't I deserve your hugs and affirmation, too?*

What happened next was nothing short of remarkable.

A gently sweet, loving, nearly audible voice whispered, "Diane, he loves you the way he knows how to love you."

I stopped dead in my tracks. Goosebumps sprang from head to toe.

Twelve words of hope had pierced the airwaves. They were more real than anything anyone had ever said to me. It was as though someone watching from far off had perfectly timed and placed a long-distance call to speak directly to the gaping hole in my heart. The sting was instantaneously reversed. As I stared at the scene before me, something shifted internally. I felt a degree of tenderness toward my dad I never had before. Somehow I was able to see him as the little boy who was abandoned by his father—the grandfather we never talked about. The grandfather I never met. The one who starved us both of his love. We shared this in common. Warm-heartedness washed over me, displaced the anger, and gave me assurance that things would be alright.

I tucked all of that into my proverbial back pocket. And you should too.

About that weekend… I gathered with dozens of other fourteen-year-olds for the anticipated retreat. For some peculiar reason, my roommate, a longtime neighbor and friend, decided to size me up as the perfect sounding board for stories about her and her much older boyfriend. Trust me, the first story alone was one too many. She admitted that she knew her escapades and the things she was doing with him were wrong. She confessed she wanted to stop but didn't know how. The whole scenario felt painfully awkward, and I hadn't a clue about how to respond.

For the life of me, I couldn't understand why she pegged me. My ears don't look like welcome mats or landing pads. And I wasn't a Miss-Know-It-All or a "Dear Abby" impostor who pretended to have all the answers. I wonder to this day why on God's green earth she thought my innocence needed a little rattling. One thing is certain: I was her captive audience Friday evening through Sunday afternoon.

All I wanted to do was skedaddle, make a break, and run for the hills. But fleeing wasn't an option. I couldn't escape her tales because I thought there was nowhere else to go. It was the perfect ambush!

I had no option other than to listen and pretend to be interested. After all, no ninth-grader wants to appear stupid or uncool. Inside my head I thought *la la la blah blah blah* to drown out every detail she was reporting. I knew with certainty that what she was describing was the kind of stuff that older, married people might do. The entire weekend was filled with cringey moments. In the end, I was worn out. I was also awakened to what another friend and her much older boyfriend were doing whenever her parents left town.

Let it be known that the only thing I confirmed and affirmed that weekend was an inner vow: *Never will I allow myself to get tangled in the kind of marathon mess she described. Never. Ever.* I wasn't tempted in the least. I had no interest in starting down a slippery slope, and I most definitely didn't want people to think I was an easy or cheap girl. I was a good girl. After all, I was growing up in a good family with a good family name. I wanted to be honorable. Compromising my reputation was the last thing I was going to do. Besides, the decision at that point was both reasonable and easy because none of the cute guys at school had shown an interest in me.

If I could go back in time, I'd tell my younger self what I've learned in my adult years: The mind is the control tower of each of our lives. All our decisions are made there. All the self-speak and all the thoughts we rehearse about relationships, successes, failures, and our sense of direction in life ultimately control us—if we let them. Like the Air Boss who controls the takeoffs and landings of jets on an aircraft carrier, we are in charge of processing and acting on our thoughts. We allow them to land and stick around or dismiss them and send them away.

Equally important is the reality that whatever happens in life, as much as it depends on us, starts in our minds. We cannot control other people, but we *can* control how we respond. How we respond is what we are accountable for.

No doubt, I struggled for years with what Joyce Meyer calls the battlefield of the mind. While I don't want to betray or distort a family and childhood I'm grateful for, I realize my family wasn't perfect. No family is. At fourteen, I didn't hate my dad—I just didn't feel the emotional connection I wanted and needed. How was I to process the bombardments of negative thoughts towards him, especially the ones that landed and lingered? The greater frustration is that I couldn't have articulated or explained my perceptions and introspections to anyone even if I had tried.

So what did I do? I opted for what was familiar. I chose to ride the emotional teeter-totter without showing my feelings or complaining. A perk of being born and raised in a time of war was knowing how to tough it out internally and be my own defender. Pushing through with the toughness of Ms. Trunchbull on the inside while projecting a perfect image like the cute and kind Matilda on the outside was easy for me. I dressed myself in pretense, dialed up and pasted a smile on my face, and marched on. I couldn't have guessed the harm in yielding to the temptation of projecting an "all's well" appearance on the exterior while ignoring the broken interior.

When fifteen-year-old me walked through the front doors of high school, arm in arm with my best friend, Sarah, I had only a shadow of an idea about who I was, who I was supposed to be, or who I would become. As I gazed down the long hallway, I was hit with a feeling of eye-watering belonging. It was instant. My heart nearly exploded with excitement about the next three years. More than anything, I wanted to cast off my mental tug-of-war and ditch the struggles with self-confidence. I was motivated to pour myself into making good grades to secure admission to a good college. I had genuine zeal for extracurriculars, cheerleading, meeting new friends, and doing whatever else it was that high school kids were supposed to do. High school for me was going to be a package deal! For the first time, too, I pictured myself with a cute boyfriend.

If anything sinister was lurking around the corner, I didn't suspect a thing. But my dad did. George Banks in *Father of the Bride* narrates the matter well:

> You fathers will understand. You have a little girl. An adorable little girl who looks up to you and adores you in a way you could never have imagined. … Next thing you know she's wearing eye shadow and high heels. From that moment on you're in a constant state of panic. You worry about her going out with the wrong kind of guys, the kind of guys who only want one thing. And you know exactly what that one thing is because it's the same thing you wanted when you were their age.[2]

Just weeks into the start of the school year, I met a tall, tan, good-looking surfer. He drove a cool jeep and had already graduated from high school, but those details were lost on me. When I introduced him to my parents, it took my dad no time to size him up. The look I saw on Dad's face as he shook the hand of this unsuspecting guy said it all. When I returned home that night, he made his disapproval explicitly firm and clear. His ability to rush to judgment stemmed not from his assignment as the Air Boss but from the job before that. Dad was a landing signal officer (LSO), and, trust me, his skills proved helpful in parenting a teenage daughter. The LSO is responsible for the safety of the aircraft and directing approaching planes to land aboard the aircraft carrier without incident. My dad was paid to be deft at making instant judgments in awkward situations. He could tell at a glance whether the plane en route to the carrier deck was too high, too low, too fast, or too slow. Using paddles, his job was to signal any needed adjustments or to call a wave-off—meaning "no landing and not now"—if the plane and pilot were in danger.

In my case, one glimpse was all it took; he called a wave-off.

As he explained the "why" behind his decision to place a halt on future dates with a much older boy, I understood he was setting a boundary. I also heard, between the lines, the unique kind of care and wisdom offered by a loving father. I wasn't thrilled with the decision, but I wasn't offended or angry either. In a weird way, his ground rules helped me feel safe and protected.

The feeling evaporated soon enough. It didn't take long to pick up on his Molly-bolt-the-doors response whenever any guy friend came to the house. At first, I thought his behavior was amusing. But then I noticed his pattern of leaving the house to tackle small jobs like cleaning the pool and washing his car or driving to the tennis court to hit balls. He'd do anything to avoid conversing with my male friends. His subconscious anxiety was palpable. Believe me when I tell you, he handled the news of my reckless driving ticket with more mercy and humor than any boy's visit. It's a wonder he didn't tear the phone book in half.

In time, it became clear that no one would win my dad's approval. I regretfully concluded it was because I couldn't either.

My father's silence, coupled with my uncertainty about whether I was even valued by him, created greater separation in our relationship and unspoken tension in our home. The disconnect was painful. I desperately needed someone to interpret me to my dad and my dad to me. I needed guidance—someone to tell me *not* to put my focus on another person as the source of healing I needed. My mother would have been my confidant, but I didn't consider involving her because it was obvious she was navigating her own issues with Dad. I found myself at a crossroads, if not a self-imposed impasse. This is the way I looked at it: I could give in and settle for a busy but ho-hum, boring life without a boyfriend, or I could set sail on all the disappointments and find my own way.

I went looking for love in all the wrong places.

I caught the proverbial big fish in eleventh grade. What started as a friendship among a group of friends quickly grew into a steady relationship to the exclusion of everyone except for my best friend, Sarah, and her boyfriend. Despite the demands on my time—studies, activities, and a job—having a big fish boyfriend was my remedy for alleviating discontent and frustration. I felt accepted, understood, and, dare I say, loved. If only I could have detected the invisible hook.

In the spring before twelfth grade, I was chosen to be co-captain of the cheering squad. It would seem to any casual observer that I was soaring—on top of the world. But low self-esteem had given way to self-focus and unhealthy compromise. Lies like *Everybody's doing it* and *You're the only one who's not* eroded my resolve. Avoiding temptation felt impossible. Headstrong and foolish, I began to make choices and cross boundaries that flew in the face of everything I swore off after that freaky confirmation retreat. I didn't know how to stop the folly. My heart was divided, and deep down, I was not in a good place. Covering up and keeping up "good girl" appearances was paramount. I have only myself to blame.

Early in my senior year, in yet another unforeseen twist, I was nominated along with two beauty pageant-worthy girls for the homecoming court. In no way, I mused, was I deserving of such an honor—much less a chance to be crowned homecoming queen. It's not that I was plucked from obscurity, but I personally believed I was way out of my league. The other girls were far more beautiful than I was, inside and out. In my mind, it wasn't even a contest—promiscuity had disqualified me. Everything inside me screamed, "You're far from royalty!"

As the school prepared for homecoming week, we cheerleaders focused on ushering in and promoting school spirit. Homecoming was a big deal at our high school: Most students participated in themed dress-up days, the football game, and the culminating celebration of a school-wide dance. Voting for the homecoming queen was an equally important part of the week. As affirmed in the opening pages of my senior yearbook, "Probably the most anticipated event of all homecoming activities involves the crowning of the queen and the presentation of her court (at the football game)." That's how it was.

My mother insisted we shop for a new dress for the occasion. We found a beautiful, blue, thin-strapped gown. She said it was the prettiest dress she had ever seen on me, so she splurged. I didn't need new shoes, but she suggested I wear her treasured Majorica pearls to complement the gown. Other than that, I didn't go overboard preparing. Juggling college applications, school, work, and time with the big fish boyfriend (now a priority) demanded my attention. Besides, a public loss neither worried nor frightened me—I expected it. My chief concern was how long it would take, after the results were announced, to leave the field to change into my cheering uniform and return to lead the squad. No one was more stunned at half-time than I was when the principal congratulated the runners-up then called my name to step forward as homecoming queen. Thunderous applause filled the stadium as the former queen placed a crystal-jeweled crown on my head. A crown! My mind was racing. Tears filled my eyes. I was shocked and humbled. *Why would they have chosen me?* I never anticipated *that* vote of confidence.

I looked toward the bleachers to find my parents. Flanked by my friends and classmates, my mom (my greatest cheerleader) was standing and waving and blowing kisses. I didn't see my father. I assumed he was talking with other parents at the concession stand and smiling and beaming with pride. But Dad wasn't at the game. He missed the entire event. My heart was hurt. I was disappointed and embarrassed. The conflict raged on—at least in my mind. I was no stranger to war, but nothing could have prepared me for the crisis ahead.

A REFLECTION

> *Dr. Henry Cloud explains the teen years as "a wonderful time of learning about the opposite sex and how to relate more intimately. They discover their bodies and feel things they have never felt before. They learn to relate in a deeper way, risking romantic attachment in a way that is much deeper than puppy love. They throw off the repression of the last decade of their lives, and they become a factory of impulses they have difficulty controlling. They also have difficulty understanding why they need to control them."[3]*

Understandably, parents avoid discussing sex with their children (because of discomfort, ignorance, or indifference). Silence, however, can become a greater enemy. What was designed and intended to be beautiful can become a place of torment or affliction. As you reflect on your adolescent years, do you remember conversations with parents or trusted adults about sex and its perfect design, or were you left to navigate those uncharted waters alone? How did this impact your sexual identity?

P.S. You are loved.

FOUR

Poised Between Peace and War

We have all done something
Dreadful in our lives,
Or have felt
The urge to.
—Wilma Derksen—

SCENT OF A WOMAN CLOSES WITH WAR VETERAN LT. COLONEL FRANK Slade praising Charlie's integrity and courage for resisting the temptation to tattle on classmates in exchange for a bribe.[1] In a passionate defense, Slade firmly asserts, "He won't sell anybody out to buy his future." He commends Charlie for taking the right path—"one made of principle that leads to character." He then pivots to his former days and, with poignant transparency, recounts: "Now I have come to the crossroads in my life. I always knew what the right path was. Without exception, I knew. But I never took it. You know why? It was too hard."[2]

Those of us who have chosen the wrong path breathe a sigh of relief. We're not alone. There's a host of us weary travelers.

We're also encouraged by Slade's honesty and openness. Perhaps we wonder how other people seemed to so effortlessly take the right road.

We are all presented with and make choices every day—sometimes dozens and sometimes hundreds. We choose when to wake up each morning. We choose what to eat, what to wear, where to work, and where to live. Some choices are significant. Some are life-changing. Others are inconsequential. Others fall somewhere in the middle of importance.

Equally valid is the fact that tests, trials, and temptations are part of the human experience. Individually and collectively, they have the potential to be the best instructors: They teach us something that no one or nothing else can. Some serve to make us better, sweeter, and more noble. Some refine, build, and strengthen us. Others make us more insistent on having our own way. Some take us out or nearly destroy us. In the words of Christine Caine, "Life will eventually turn every person upside down and inside out. No one is immune."[3]

What happens when troubles and hardship sideswipe us? Our reactions—healthy or unhealthy—ultimately depend on answers to questions like these: How well do we know ourselves? Do we have family and friends to scaffold us in our time of need? How sensitive is our conscience? How deeply rooted are our convictions and principles? Are our hearts grounded in confidence and truth or in fear and lies? Are we prone to run or throw temper tantrums?

By no means is this an exhaustive list of inquiry. I offer it as a sampling of the slew of questions running through our minds—especially as we look in the rearview mirror and try to make sense of why we turned left at the fork in the road and didn't make a U-turn. Each of our stories is as unique as our thumbprint or the iris of our eye. Our ability to explore and to understand our past will help us to re-examine unhealthy choices and damaging behaviors. In turn, we will be strengthened, renewed in the hope that true and lasting change is possible, and motivated to take positive steps forward. Each of our lives truly is more valuable, filled with greater purpose, and more worthy of love and connectedness than we can imagine.

I've learned that circumstances in our childhood are oftentimes key to understanding how we answer these kinds of questions. In other words, if we can examine our formative years with a fresh commitment to honesty, intentional vulnerability, and courage, we often discover the reasons underlying our less-than-honorable and destructive decisions during our teens (and beyond). Life begins to make more sense when what was once covered is disclosed and what was once hidden is revealed. Looking back helps us move forward and into healing. In the words of Henry David Thoreau, "It's not what you look at that matters, it's what you see."[4]

I've shared that during my childhood my mother was devoted, caring, and present. What I wanted and needed more of was quality time with my father. I loved him and was grateful for the time he gave me, but I often felt overlooked and forsaken because of his multiple deployments. In my teenage years, there was little fun, laughter, and enjoying life together. When in town, he was emotionally unavailable and absorbed in his work, sports, and hobbies. It was easy to conclude that he just didn't love me as much or value me as much. My assessment wasn't true, but I perceived it to be true. To a kid, perception is everything. It doesn't take math smarts to know "time + love = value."

Dr. M. Scott Peck validates this: "The time and quality of time parents devote to their children indicate the degree to which they are valued by their parents. ... Children who are truly loved unconsciously know themselves to be valued. ... When children know that they are valued ... they then feel valuable. ... The feeling of being valuable—'I am a valuable person'—is a direct product of parental love."[5]

Feelings of emptiness, loss of attachment, gnawing insecurity, disconnect, and loneliness were my reality. What I didn't know and couldn't identify was that these feelings were symptomatic of what the authors of *Unraveled Roots* refer to as abandonment. They explain that every human requires the love, security, and connection of both parents to thrive. If these ingredients are present and the parent/child relationship bond is close, the child's confidence and security are established. She develops a healthy view of herself.

On the other hand, if the relationship with either or both parents is damaged or lacks any or all of the beneficial, life-giving ingredients, the child is prone to feelings of abandonment. The emotional disconnect often results in low self-worth, and she can unconsciously bring that effect into adolescence and adulthood. To numb the pain and fill the internal or external sense of emptiness and loss, she may enter into unhealthy relationships with friends and engage in risky behaviors. While parents can provide everything needed to survive, we need full heart involvement to thrive. "*Knowing* we're loved in our heads and *feeling* we're loved in our hearts are two very different things."[6]

Good grief! I wish I would have known then what I know now. No wonder I went looking for love, significance, and validation.

Shortly after the crowning moment of my life, everything returned to normal. The school year moved forward and was turbulence-free and uneventful. Sarah and I received acceptance letters to the same college, and with high school graduation less than two months away, we were giddy planning for our freshman year. Rooming together would be a highlight. Our future and all the possibilities that lay ahead looked bright.

The big fish boyfriend was still very much in the picture, but one obvious dilemma was bubbling to the surface. College would put miles between us. We'd be hours away from one another. I'd be moving to another city. He thought I'd be moving to another galaxy. He tried his best to dissuade me from going away to school. I concluded the idea was preposterous! I stood firm insisting I'd soon be on my way. Everyone in my family had a college degree or would have one in the not-too-distant future.

It was a season of decisions—the normal, easy, everyday types. Which path? Which road? Dr. Seuss offers winsome wisdom:

You'll look up and down streets. Look 'em over with care.
>About some you will say, 'I don't choose to go there.'
>With your head full of brains and your shoes full of feet,
>you're too smart to go down any not-so-good street.
>And you may not find *any*
>you'll want to go down.
>In that case, of course,
>you'll head straight out of town.[7]

Head full of brains? Check. Shoes full of feet? Check. Heading out of town? Check. And then. That thing that was never supposed to happen to me happened to me.

I was pregnant.

With one stormy, shocking bolt, my life turned upside down and inside out. I was cast into a world of isolation, walled in, and overtaken by existential panic. This wasn't any part of my anticipated path and plan.

My initial thoughts seemed reasonable. *Pregnant? What happened? Pregnant? There must be some mistake. Pregnant? I couldn't be. How could I be? Pregnant? Not me. How did I get here? What do I do?*

Then my imagination ran riot. The focus shifted. Fear and condemnation gripped me. A relentless onslaught of accusations harassed my mind: *Pregnant? Look what you've done now. Pregnant? How stupid. You're on your own now. Pregnant? Your parents will be so disappointed. Pregnant? What about college? Everyone goes to college. Pregnant? What shame you'll bring to yourself and to your entire family. Pregnant? You better figure it out and fix it. Fast. PREGNANT?*

I called Sarah, my dependable confidant. "What are you going to do?" she asked.

We both cried.

Fear and condemnation gave way to suffocating anguish. I was terrified, numb, and spinning out of control. *Look-what-you've-done* torment exacts instant isolation. My mind was in such turmoil that I wasn't even thinking in a normal way. My vision became clouded. All

I could see was the torrential storm of disappointment and embarrassment I'd unleash on my family and the humiliation they'd endure. *Isn't it better to preserve the reputation of the "all-American family" and the "good girl"?*

Indeed, the shame and the accompanying distress of promiscuity and an out-of-wedlock pregnancy would call attention to the fact that I was not who I wanted to be or who I appeared to be. I was out of balance and scared for the mask to be pulled back. For people to know my secret conduct and the messed-up me—the girl who had followed her nose, had chosen temporary pleasures and self-gratification, and had blurred the lines. "The tyranny of public opinion can manipulate our lives," writes Brennan Manning, *"What will the neighbors think? What will my friends think?* The expectations of others can exert a subtle but controlling pressure on our behavior."[8]

I was also stuck in a moral pickle. Pregnancy brings forth a new life—a human baby. I had read *Horton Hears a Who!* The statement, "A person's a person, no matter how small," trumpeted between my ears.[9] But I wasn't ready for parenthood. I wanted to go back in time. I needed control so my life would unfold as planned.

From left field dropped a hazy memory of a radio commercial I had once heard for a place called Hillcrest. *I think it mentioned "unwanted pregnancy."* Something outside of me—something unseen, something subtle, something that sounded very real—seemed to be exerting influence and stoking the fire of my inner turmoil. I hadn't talked about the advertisement with anyone. I was clueless about what they did there. There was no need to know—til now. *Could they "fix" this pregnancy?* Believe me, if sex wasn't a topic for conversation at the family dinner table, you can bet abortion and abortion clinics weren't either. *Why has this commercial surfaced?* Tom Sawyer's wisdom knocked at the door of my heart, "Right is right, and wrong is wrong, and a body ain't got no business doing wrong when he ain't ignorant and knows better."[10]

I picked up the phone book, scanned through it, and found the number and address of the clinic. If only my dad had torn that phone book in half back when I was in eleventh grade.

I paused. *Am I truly giving this option consideration? Aren't I too smart to go down any not-so-good street? Am I willing to sell someone out to buy my future?*

Unbending, uninvited thoughts also rolled in with greater frequency. *Go ahead. Call. You're tough. Don't waste time. You can get on with your normal life—a fun life, free of shame and judgment. This will be your secret. Forever. No one will know. All the plans for your future will be safe.*

The place of testing and trials is gnarly. There are straight paths. There are crossroads. There are slippery roads. Then there are crises. I was in a full-blown crisis—poised between peace and war. Oh, the agony in the valley of indecision.

Dr. Peck notes crises as "generally points in our lives where we are faced with a tough decision, a decision whose outcome will determine how our lives go thereafter for better or ill."[11] I tried to visualize my future. Blank. Blank. Blanker. Nothing was clear except a dark path. I couldn't see around the corner. I couldn't see a way out. I had lost my strength and sense of value and truly believed my only choice was to be either a student or a mother. My vision was too far blurred to know this was a false choice. I also felt a very heavy and real presence nudging, if not driving, me toward a decision I never imagined or believed I would face. *What if this route brings relief?*

"Most women," explains Dr. Theresa Burke, "choose abortion out of fear that carrying their unplanned pregnancy to term will deprive them of a wanted relationship, the approval of others, their education, a career, or some other desired goal. Many people mistakenly assume that no woman has an abortion if she does not want one. In fact, while many women believe they *need* one, very few, if any, *want* one."[12]

She quotes feminist Frederica Mathewes-Green who wrote, "No woman wants an abortion as she wants an ice cream cone or a Porsche. She wants an abortion as an animal caught in a trap wants to gnaw off its own leg. Abortion is a tragic attempt to escape a desperate situation by an act of violence and self-loss. Abortion is not a sign that women are free but a sign that they are desperate."[13]

For this desperate seventeen-year-old girl, terminating the

pregnancy seemed practical, not something I wanted. It was *most definitely not* something I *wanted*. Burke continues, "For most women, abortion is more likely to be perceived as an 'evil necessity.' Many women feel completely overwhelmed by their situation. Under such pressures, many will rush into an abortion without ever examining the full range of their beliefs, needs, and feelings."[14]

With my back against the wall, I was utterly convinced I didn't have the time nor the wisdom to work through my moral dilemma, sift through possible consequences, or explore better options. Frankly, my radar screen was void of any viable alternative. Only in hindsight is my mismanagement of the situation so baffling. One of my beloved aunts had had her baby outside of marriage. Unfortunately, no one shared details of her situation when we were young. Nobody mentioned to the younger generation, "In case of emergency, please know, we keep our babies. We're here for you. We'll stand together with you through thick and thin." All I knew was that my precious cousin didn't grow up in the same household with her father. The idea of following in my aunt's footsteps, asking for help and support, and keeping the baby never entered my mind.

I faced a fierce internal conflict—the most intense fight of my life. The clock was ticking away, and the pressure to settle the nagging, no-win decision was extreme. There was no middle of the road or halfway measure. I felt worn down and weak. Self-pity and the urge to quit were winning. The big fish boyfriend was equally concerned. He tried to express his opinions. They went in one ear and out the other; self-reliance was in overdrive. Believing I didn't have a choice, I crumbled. I placed the call, scheduled the appointment, and called Sarah to enlist her help. I truly felt I was doing the best I could, given the circumstances.

Sarah and I had known each other since we were four years old. We were best friends— closer than sisters—and could count on each other through thick and thin. Joined at the hip and bound for college, we were good girls with good grades. We were members of the National Honor Society. Neither of us had a single blemish of misbehavior or discipline on our school records. We hadn't even skipped school on senior skip day, a decision that played in our favor. When we requested a well-deserved, personal day off from school to go shopping, our mothers, without hesitation and oblivious to the undercurrent, happily granted our pleas.

That spring day was my day of clouds and darkness—the day I was wounded in the war. Actually, "wounded" doesn't come close to describing the fallout. There was absolutely nothing superficial about it. The condensed misery of such an experience is more than the human imagination can absorb or digest.

On the other side of what many claim to be a "simple procedure," a "non-event," a "no big deal," I emerged feeling that I had barely escaped the most shell-shocking, soul-wrenching, heartbreaking trauma on the planet. I hadn't just had my tonsils surgically removed, skinned my knee, or stubbed my toe. There was nothing easy or routine about it. It was certainly more than a "non-event."

I was all at once terribly alone, three hundred dollars poorer, and spiritually bankrupt. I felt a chasm open wide and a separation from I didn't know what. The alienation was real, but I had neither a word nor a storehouse of words to describe the depth of this emptiness and estrangement. The finality and pain of such transgression and iniquity is so difficult to accept.

Every one of my five senses was affected. I was alive, and yet my innermost being felt shattered beyond comprehension. Bitter pangs of conscience kicked in immediately. A blitzkrieg of mental torment stormed in, pummeling whatever strength remained. Here's what I heard: *Oh, you idiot. How stupid. Look what you've done now. Who do you think you are? You took the life of your child. Now you're really on your own. You have to hide it. You can't tell anyone what you did. No one will like you. No one can know. How could you have done this? You should feel ashamed. That was wrong. You're guilty. You're bad.*

I rehearsed the arsenal of thoughts over and over again believing wholeheartedly it was true. The only difference between me on this battlefield and a soldier injured in war is that I alone was responsible for unleashing the firestorm. I was overcome with grief, the identical emotional response I was forced to contend with when Navy friends and my grandfather died. In my mind, I had made one huge, irrevocable, unforgivable mistake—the unpardonable sin. In the words of another woman who chose to terminate her pregnancy, "I left the clinic and felt sure that hell would open up and swallow me."[15]

Crippled by shame and shrouded in silence and secrecy, I strangled a sob, bottled my emotions, and hobbled out of Hillcrest forever changed. The words of Lt. Colonel Frank Slade ring true: "There is nothing like the sight of an amputated spirit. There is no prosthetic for that."[16]

The big fish boyfriend visited later that day to check on me. I could hardly face him. The sting of moral failure and acute grief have that effect. Shipwrecked and barely breathing but propped up by autopilot stoicism, the only words I could assemble went something like this: "That was *the most painful* experience of my life. I *never ever ever* want to talk about it again. *Ever.*" He seemed to understand. Tears flowed. In hindsight, he was nursing his own personal grief, but I was tied in a knot of selfish concern and ignorance, drowning in my own sorrow and despair. I didn't have the emotional bandwidth to deal with his pain. The reality was that he, too, experienced a loss. No doubt, the tentacles of my choice had already begun to spread and choke others.

The conversation ended quickly. I felt as empty as a pocket. It was afternoon on the first day of the rest of my life.

A REFLECTION

The authors of Unraveled Roots *share that real-life stories are profitable for helping us to begin to understand more about how our past has shaped us and sets us up for the choices we've made and continue to make. "The goal is never to go back and assign blame," they write. "The goal is to go back and look at what shaped you so you can learn from it, understand the 'why' behind those choices, and start the forgiveness and healing process."[17] Admitting our past (even to ourselves) is the first step to breaking the power of silence and secrecy that holds us captive. Taking this jump off the starting block is the beginning of healing for our broken hearts and for our physical and emotional pains and sorrows.*

P.S. You are loved.

FIVE

The Wilderness

Sometimes when you lose your way,
you find YOURSELF.
—Mandy Hale—

MOSES. HAVE YOU EVER HEARD OF HIM? I WAS INTRODUCED TO THIS seemingly larger-than-life leader of Red Sea fame years before the cable television boom and YouTube. While flipping through the three major network channels sometime around Easter and Passover, I stumbled across Cecile B. DeMilles's movie, *The Ten Commandments*. It has aired annually since its inaugural prime-time broadcast in 1973, the year of the Roe v. Wade decision.[1] I knew absolutely nothing about Moses—neither his name nor his story. After discovering him through this film, I made it my annual tradition to watch it.

Mesmerized by his infant rescue story, courage, and deep voice, I was glued to every word and gripped by every scene. That he was raised as an adopted son in the splendor and privilege of a palace yet chose to side with his people and lead them out of slavery fascinated me. Supernatural events—his staff becoming a cobra and the sea becoming a highway—grabbed my attention. A fan of underdogs, I cheered as Moses and his people crossed onto dry land while walls of water collapsed on the pursuing army. The entire movie is filled with interest and intrigue.

One scene remained a curiosity for years: Moses's punishment after he comes to the aid of a fellow Hebrew and kills Pharaoh's master builder. When his actions come to light, he is removed from civilized Egypt, given a robe, a staff, and one day's supply of bread and water before being banished to the desert. Even as a kid, I understood the concept of consequences, prison, and prisoners of war, but the idea of forcing a man to survive by himself in a vast wasteland baffled me. The narrator's doomy voice addresses the severity of the moment:

> Into the blistering wilderness of Shur, the man who walked with kings now walks alone. Torn from the pinnacle of royal power, stripped of all rank and earthly wealth. A forsaken man without a country. Without a hope. His soul in turmoil like the hot winds and raging sands that lash him with the fury of a taskmaster's whip. He is driven forward, always forward, by a God unknown, for the land unseen. Into the molten wilderness … each night brings the black embrace of loneliness. In the mocking whisper of the wind, he hears the echoing voices of the dark. His tortured mind wondering if they call the memory of past trials or wail foreboding of disasters yet to come.[2]

Alone. Forsaken. Without hope. Soul in turmoil. The land unseen. Black embrace of loneliness. Mocking whisper. Echoing voices of the dark. Tortured mind. Disasters yet to come. In plain language, haven't those of us who have experienced an abortion felt the gut kick and foreboding weight of being cast out? We couldn't have envisioned this in our lives, but after "the event," we find ourselves in similar territory: the badlands. We know what it feels like to walk in Moses's sandals— slaves of a cruel taskmaster driving us into a harsh wilderness.

We wonder if we will ever move forward. Will we survive? Will we ever thrive?

"None of us," writes Eugene Peterson, "lives in a continuously ordered, protected, safe, confident world of accomplishment, basking in admiration. Accident or anger—I'll add abortion—breaks in upon us, and we run for our lives. We run to the wilderness."[3]

Peterson calls this not a *geographical* wilderness but a *circumstantial* wilderness. We flee to it because the anguish, despair, and tormenting thoughts that drove us to choose abortion don't just go away and disappear afterward. They amplify. They multiply. To our surprise, the emotional roller coaster and all but one of the problems we thought would be solved and settled intensify. David Reardon shares, "They become sources of constant reflection or stifling avoidance. They can even become the source of crippling self-condemnation."[4]

We bargained for autonomy but gained pain and oppression.

Navigating in ignorance and blindness, we cross from one realm of shock and awe into another equally foreign and dark stretch. Our wilderness expands. We continue to feel the misery of abortion's sting. The act we counted on to bring us so-called freedom destroyed freedom. It's a catch-22. A well-designed fishing lure. Even when it appeared to be the right choice, only after the lure had been swallowed did we discover it was the wrong choice.[5] For many women, the distress is magnified and made more complicated because, after all, there's no going back. Like all repressed facts, the death of our child keeps disturbing us, haunting us, and draining our hope. Before long, we believe we have no hope.

We long to be in Dorothy's cute red shoes—holding our cute dog, tapping our heels, and trusting that eventually everything works out fine. *Will it? Ever?*

When I woke up early on the morning of the second day of the rest of my life, I heard the call of the wild. I was in the great unknown. For me, it was like Buck's first day—a nightmare. I identified with the feeling of being suddenly jerked from the heart of civilization and flung into the heart of things primordial. There was neither peace nor rest nor a moment's safety. All was confusion and action. I felt an imperative need, consciously and subconsciously, to be constantly alert.[6]

Everything seemed surreal. I couldn't look up. I couldn't look out. I was downcast and inward-focused and on heightened alert.

No one at the clinic had provided advanced warning or prepared me for the impending emotional sting. There were no pre-op counseling sessions or medical forms or pamphlets shouting anything along the lines of STEEP DESCENT, FALLING ROCKS, or HEARTBREAK DEAD AHEAD. There were no post-op instructions on how to cope: *You may feel regret and sadness—like the walls have closed in on you. You may feel dull and diminished. You may suffer the bitter pangs of conscience. You may not sleep well. This is normal. You may feel lonely, but you're not alone. Seek out a trusted friend or speak with a professional if you feel too unsettled.*

On the post-operative side, there was no bereavement counseling to suggest that grieving the loss was healthier than pretending the child never lived, let alone died. There was neither mention nor discussion about what might lie ahead. For that matter, there were no encouraging signs or directions that might point to an off-ramp. No one gave the slightest indication that somewhere I might find a trail of breadcrumbs to lead me out of the dark forest.

Minute by minute, I struggled with fog and confusion: *Why can't I stop thinking about it? This is far heavier than what I signed up for. How can I get out from under this rock?* I reached for what was familiar—the strategy that played hand-in-glove with the rugged independence and stoicism I learned as a child. Assuming I was strong and capable of handling problems and disappointments without complaint—even one this size—I resolved to bear the heavy load myself and push through the pain. Silently. It was the logical, easy, and sensible answer. *After all, I deserve it.* In Charles Dickens's words, "We forge the chains we wear in life."[7]

Brushing it off as though I had a tooth extraction the day before, I buckled up my proverbial seatbelt, pasted on a happy, clappy kind of smile, and off to school I went.

An important point, as naive as it may sound, is that I didn't suspect that other girls in my school or neighborhood or anyone else I knew had experienced abortion. My friends and I didn't talk openly about private matters like sex. Much less a crisis pregnancy. At least in my bubble, it was taboo. Before my dilemma, I never once heard or had a conversation about the procedure. This exacerbated my feeling of isolation before I stepped foot into school that morning.

As I approached my locker and began to mingle with friends and classmates (the ones who, months earlier, considered me worthy of wearing a crystal-jeweled crown), something more pernicious than the horror of the previous day's damage took hold. My imagination raced. Suddenly I was Hester Prynne from Nathaniel Hawthorne's *The Scarlet Letter,* stepping from a Puritan jail into the open air wearing a token similar to the one that adorned her chest. The difference? Her "A," embellished with fine red cloth, elaborate embroidery, and gold threads, adorned the breast of her gown for the world to see. My "A" was branded on my heart. Invisible. Yet the stigma had a similar venomous impact. To borrow Hawthorne's words, "It had the effect of a spell, taking me out of the ordinary relations with humanity, and enclosing me in a sphere by myself."[8]

Royalty had become riffraff. The commoner wanted to throw away her crystal-jeweled crown. I was crumbling and experiencing in real-time the words of Michel de Montaigne, "On the highest throne in the world, we still sit only on our own bottom."[9] Fear that my day of infamy might be exposed both threatened and paralyzed me. Having to endure the kind of scorn and ridicule heaped on Hester terrified me. I determined, once and for all, to block everything from my mind, bury "the event" six feet deep, and leave it there for the rest of my life— never to be exhumed.

Hoping to have salvaged something—or anything—resembling the normal seventeen-year-old me, I jumped back into everyday life. We're all escape artists, aren't we?

Admittedly, soldiering through day-to-day life in my own strength worked in the early steps of my blistering wilderness experience. Graduation, the summer job, the move to a new town, and the first few weeks of the college routine proved to be helpful distractions. Miles beyond that, however, my creative survival efforts waned. A new range of emotions settled in. I struggled with melancholy and sleepless nights. I developed an unfamiliar, less than half-hearted interest in learning. Concentrating on my studies was difficult. No doubt, my initiative and drive had been undermined. Despite being among thousands of people, I felt alone. I experimented in secular remedies like over-sampling at late-night parties and binging and purging—thank goodness neither of these coping mechanisms became a stronghold.

Abortion is a searing experience. The crazy thing is that I didn't—I couldn't—connect the dots between "the event" and the complexities of my overall well-being or lack thereof. The cause of my malaise wasn't at all obvious.

Symptoms of depression like lethargy, sadness, disorganization, and disconnection appeared. Unease and conflict in my relationships erupted—especially with Sarah. All the squabbling was unhealthy, but, subconsciously and in desperation, I tried to hold on to her friendship like no other: She knew too much. The stress and strain took its toll, and, sadly, our friendship ended before summer vacation. I had no idea what was going on inside me. I was a mystery to myself. My internal world—my emotions and thoughts both incoming and outgoing—was one big, boiling jumble which continued to ebb and flow throughout my college experience.

Fortunately, after transitioning into the season of being a responsible adult, the inner dread reduced to a slow simmer. It hadn't evaporated, though, because inevitably something would bubble up reconnecting me to that horrible day. Every spring, for instance, when the anniversary of "the event" approached, I'd feel the slow squeeze of anxiety. I even added a few blocks to my afternoon commute to avoid seeing the apartment complex that shared the same ghastly name of the clinic. Anything to avoid the suffocating disappointment of my decision and with myself. At some point—I can't exactly recall when or how—I experienced a kind of breakthrough. I stopped remembering and resumed living, somewhere between surviving and thriving. Underneath, I was a walking civil war.

The loudest voices insist abortion is a safe and common health intervention. They assert physical risks and emotional and psychological harm are rare. They downplay our grief, leading us to feel abnormal for experiencing it. Others, unwavering in their claim that the medical procedure is easy and routine, emphatically declare ill effects are non-existent. Mum's the word from people secluded in ivory towers and positions of influence: abortion clinics, medical offices, government offices, high school and university student counseling centers, mental health offices, psychiatry and psychology associations, public health researchers and investigators, corporations, and churches. Please pardon the candid opinion, but by and large, they treat the whole abortion fallout with popcorn and folding chairs—as if there's no consequence at all. No harm, no foul. Nada.

The powers that be go to great lengths to downplay physical risks to the mother, but short and long-term abortion-related injuries are real. Even the prolific abortion doctor Warren Hern, admits in his book *Abortion Practices,* "In medical practice, there are few surgical procedures given so little attention and so underrated in its potential hazards as abortion. It is a commonly held view that complications are inevitable."[10] In a pro-woman culture, no woman, pre or post-abortion, should be denied the right to know about reliable medical studies that highlight complications such as pelvic inflammatory disease, placenta previa, ectopic pregnancies, and uterine perforation. These injuries and others can lead to future problems.

If emotional reactions were common, the intelligentsia note that we'd have an epidemic of women seeking psychological treatment. They refuse to admit, at least publicly, that abortion leads to suffering —physically, spiritually, emotionally, or psychologically. They claim substantive studies have found abortion to be a relatively benign procedure in terms of emotional effect. Any scientific studies that show negative mental health outcomes are characterized as flawed.[11] These dissenting studies are also retracted or scrubbed from medical journals.

My story and yours, more than likely, would be rejected as fabrications, inventions, and tactical contrivances. You get the point.

Imagine making the big decision to reach out to a college counselor or any number of other licensed, professional therapists about your anxiety, relationships, insomnia, or depression. It's highly unlikely you'd be asked about a pregnancy or abortion. But imagine having the courage to mention the abortion and receiving a response that sounds something like this: "There's no evidence to support that your symptoms have anything to do with abortion." Or "Your symptoms are not a big deal." Or "Your symptoms are probably tied to previous psychological problems."

Dr. Miriam Grossman, a stalwart advocate of women and truth-teller about the trauma of abortion, shares her observations and remarks about an online forum (www.afterabortion.com) where "women provide to one another what psychology does not: a forum to share experiences, a place to find validation, support, and advice." Of the women seeking and exchanging help and support on the site, she writes, "As a psychiatrist … I see in these women what I see in many of my patients—exceptional strength and courage. They continue to function, even with all their hideous flashbacks and raw emotions. Somehow they go to school and work, cook meals, drive carpool. To me, they are heroines, no less than anyone else who gets up each day with a broken spirit and heart and finds a way to survive."[12]

It's puzzling that abortion studies presenting evidence of a link between abortion and negative outcomes—particularly mental health and substance abuse disorders—are rejected as unreliable, inaccurate, misleading, and invalid. It's equally perplexing that even small studies showing abortion's detrimental effects on women are often "explained away" or swept under the proverbial rug—no matter if the symptoms are long-lasting or short-lived (initial guilt, regrets, and sensitivity to abortion-related comments).

A book titled *The Turnaway Study* highlights a study of the outcomes of one thousand women who were recruited shortly after having an early or a just-in-time abortion and women whose pregnancies exceeded gestational limits and were denied an abortion.

The book details their responses to multiple choice questions and open-ended questions and profiles ten women and their stories in their own words.

In what *New York Times Magazine* calls "the most rigorous" study, the principal investigator looked at whether women develop mental health problems following an abortion.[13] The study, labeled "landmark" and "groundbreaking" by other popular news sources and major media outlets, tracked the participants to compare the mental health and well-being and economic outcomes of those who had an abortion and those who did not. Her conclusion? Abortion is not associated with mental health problems and women who are denied them fare worse in areas of health, finances, and family than women who receive them.

In a YouTube video, the principal investigator reveals that the women were recruited over three years and contacted for five years via semi-annual telephone interviews. She admits there were *no* in-person interviews. She explains why abortion, based on her study, is *not* a mental health issue: "The whole context of their lives so outweighs this one event. I don't think people, once they have an abortion, their identity is 'abortion person.' I think they move on. It's not a huge effect, but it's there. Mostly people are extremely resilient." In direct response to the interviewer's question, "Does abortion hurt women?" she responds that she and her team of researchers looked at mental health (a plethora of mental health outcomes, including depression, anxiety, post-traumatic stress, and suicidality) over time and found "no evidence that abortion is associated with worse mental health outcomes." She then concludes, "Our whole social commentary around abortion is so infused with stigma that people imagine it's a much worse event than it is."[14]

The study received accolades because of its yearslong time frame and the size of its representative sample. So it's worth pausing, at the risk of wading into something that seems too technical, to consider this study at face value, especially in light of the fact there have been over sixty-three *million* reported abortions in the U.S. alone since 1973.[15] I told you that you're not alone! Let's compare this number and time frame (over fifty years) with the size of The Turnaway Study—one thousand women procured over three years and followed for five years. Assuming a lower-than-average nine hundred thousand abortions each year, a conservative estimate of 2.7 million women experienced abortion in the time it took just to recruit these women. An estimated 4.5 million women experienced abortion in the five years it took to follow them.

I applaud the efforts and investment of time and energy of these researchers, but The Turnaway Study raises a significant question. Is it sincere—in the age of trusting science and upholding scientific integrity and rigor—to extrapolate the data of a short-term, five-year study of one thousand women who represent only 0.037% of the total abortion population (during the three-year procurement of women) and conclude there's "no evidence that abortion is associated with worse mental health outcomes?" What about the effects ten, twenty, or forty years later? What about the other 2.699 million women who were not part of the three-year procurement and study? What about the other 62.999 million U.S. women who have experienced abortion since 1973?

A more reasonable conclusion is that it's nearly impossible for voices like this to admit that choosing abortion is like going against the law of gravity—the consequence is bruises and broken bones.[16] Perhaps the truth is just too horrifying to admit. Even for them.

Did a nurse or doctor—anyone—tell you that aside from some "possible discomfort, cramping, or pain" you might grapple with adverse effects and intense feelings of despair, loss, and gloom? What about the inherent sorrow and grief associated with human loss? Were you encouraged to talk with a friend or counselor to discuss and process these feelings? Did anyone, at the very least, suggest that it's common to try to repress or ignore details to keep the pain at bay? That your eating habits might change? That you might be tempted to self-medicate with addictive substances? Was there anybody in your life who told the truth that you might be haunted by a shouting conscience and long-term what-ifs? Did anyone sound the warning that you might struggle with daily life long after?

Be gentle with yourself. The likely answer is a big, fat, ginormous, resounding *NO!* The silence is deafening.

To be sure, every woman responds uniquely to her experience. No two women show the same constellation of symptoms. Our reactions are as different as our beliefs, imperfections, and strengths. They're as distinct as the individuals who drove us to the clinics and the doctors who performed the abortions.

Some women have no qualms. They're able to nurse their decision, muffle their conscience, and then re-enter life with an "I'm fine!" kind of approach. While they claim to be relieved and symptom-free, I suspect they haven't escaped the consequences of that decision. Not ultimately, anyhow. We become experts in avoidance. Theresa Burke, who helps women recover joy in their lives after abortion, says, "The subject of abortion is so objectionable and anxiety-laden that we choose to avoid the issue at all costs."[17]

I'm mindful of and sympathetic toward countless women on the other end of the spectrum—those who were persuaded not to keep their babies because of malformations. I weep for those who were forced to choose abortion and those whose backstories may include a deeper, more tangled web of unspeakable trauma like abuse, neglect, or trafficking. For them, the abortion wound is the lid on Pandora's box. To open it up would unleash deep, dark, painful memories of the devil's lair. Reopening those unbearable scars requires someone to hold their hand and lovingly guide them. My heart is tender for them.

Another group of women I've found in my research and observations and in my personal life are those who boast no ill effects. They are perfectly willing to dig in their heels and die on this hill. They proclaim their conscience doesn't shout. I submit these are the women who refuse to come to terms with what they've experienced. They are often the most adamant, opinionated, unbending, strident, blustering, and prideful women. They've built impenetrable walls around themselves. I have great compassion for them.

The more plausible and perhaps more credible story is that negative reactions to abortion aren't as rare and benign as even the "best studies" claim. The truth is, we've been fed a raft of misinformation. There is mounting evidence and an ever-expanding cadre of sympathetic and compassionate professionals who agree that most women don't just "move on." At least not for long. As Jodi Picoult says, "Once you throw a stone, there are ripples in the pond, even if you remove the rock."[18]

Women on the battlefield are plagued, at a minimum, with pain, regret, and remorse. We muddle along with bitter tears of self-reproach and self-hatred. We punish ourselves. We punish others. I'd be remiss if I didn't mention that the pendulum of side effects swings wide—all the way to infertility, self-harm, and suicide. We remain tight-lipped. We suffer silently. Consciously and subconsciously. We assume that banishment to the wilderness is a boundless, eternal life sentence. Overnight or over time, we become proficient at suppressing our emotions.

Or so we think.

Memories resurface. Dreams break in like a brook gurgling over stones in an otherwise calm and steady stream. While the outward appearance might not be in shambles like Humpty Dumpty after his fall, our true, inner self struggles: *When will the angst subside? Will the mental cramping and wounds ever abate? Why can't I shake this? Is there any hope of putting the pieces back together again?*

There's no stopwatch for the struggle and drudgery. We cudgel our brains for a solution.

Considering that the U.S. averages one million reported abortions each year and one in four women choose abortion, valid questions surface: Where are these women? Why are so few people willing to admit that abortion might be an event that sows wind and confusion into our lives? Why do we turn a deaf ear and a blind eye to post-abortion stress, suffering, and damage? Why is any woman left alone to navigate the wilderness…completely ignorant about volatile postabortion emotions, destructive behaviors, and ramifications of poor choices?

If I didn't know any better, I would suggest that pushing or believing the no harm, no foul narrative is patent, intellectual honesty. If I didn't know any better, I'd insist the narrative isn't laced with an air of sinister intentionality. Ah—the foolishness of the wise. By consequence, millions upon millions of women are forced to aimlessly wander in the wilderness, carrying the gnawing, heavy load of prolonged grief, confusion, restlessness, and guilt.

I often think about a dear friend's mother who, at ninety-two years old, still worries she's unworthy to receive forgiveness for the abortion she had in college. She admits she has never stopped thinking about her experience and that time hasn't been powerful enough to heal her unease. I admire her honesty and wonder about the women who continue to live in a charade of nonchalance.

No harm? No hurt? No damage? Pure fiction. Something welling up from the depths of the human heart cries for somebody to expose the voices that insist, "Pay no attention to the truth behind the curtain!"

If you're a woman who's still zigzagging across the wilderness, take heart. One fast-growing, national non-profit specializing in post-abortion care shines the light on why the majority of women don't seek help: 90% of people impacted by abortion don't know where to go for healing.[19] With empathy and understanding, friends at Support After Abortion are countering misinformation and falsehoods with facts and more facts. They're validating women's feelings, identifying resources, and openly sharing where women can find judgment-free assistance for help in overcoming a past abortion experience.

This group is only part of a growing chorus of sister soldiers who have been on the battlefield and in the wilderness. The ripple effect of information spoken through the airwaves and on platforms and websites is helping women discover and admit that our pain and sorrow were not and are not a figment of our imaginations. We know better. We're not crazy or weird or delusional. We can validate that women are hurting because we've survived the trauma of abortion *and* its deleterious consequences. The message of hope is a truthful message, even if it's not corroborated by daily press releases, news reports, social media posts, and "respected" academic and medical journals

We also know that the wilderness doesn't have to be a boundless, eternal life sentence. In the spirit of sisterhood, we long for you to be free from oppression. We want *every* woman to be fully alive—living her best life, gracefully and beautifully.

A REFLECTION

"The circumstantial wilderness," writes Eugene Peterson, "is a terrible, frightening, and dangerous place; but I also believe that it's a place of beauty. There are things to be seen, heard, and experienced in this wilderness that can be seen, heard, and experienced nowhere else. When we find ourselves in the wilderness, we do well to be frightened; we also do well to be alert, open-eyed. In the wilderness we're plunged into an awareness of danger and death; at the very same moment we're plunged, if we let ourselves be, into an awareness of the great mystery of God and the extraordinary preciousness of life."[20]

All of us are given moments, days, months, or years of exile. What will we do with them? Wish we were someplace else? Complain? Escape into fantasies? Drug ourselves into oblivion? Or will we build and plant and marry? Will we seek and find the shalom (peace, wholeness, health, well-being) of the place we inhabit and the people we are with? Exile reveals what really matters and frees us to pursue what really matters, which is to seek God with all our hearts.[21]

P.S. You are loved.

SIX

Rescue Begins

Now every time I witness a strong person,
I want to know
What darkness did you conquer
In your story? Mountains do not rise
Without earthquakes.
—Katherine MacKenett—

HAVE YOU EVER DREAMED THAT YOUR LIFE MIGHT BE PART OF A FAR bigger, far grander, and far more important story? Have you ever imagined there may be more to your life than what you know in the realm of your five senses? Perhaps you've entertained the idea of a greater reality—as in, "There's *got* to be more!" The movie *The Truman Show* is the quintessential allegory that helps us conceptualize such thoughts.[1]

Truman Burbank is the unwitting star of a live reality television program called *The Truman Show.* Broadcast day and night, the show is a carefully crafted and controlled production of Cristof, the show's creator, executive producer, and chief antagonist. Truman is living an artificial reality in front of hidden cameras in the fabricated seaside town of Seahaven Island. Everything in his life is manufactured—the weather, the noonday sun, the stars, and the moon. The residents, his family, and his friends are all paid actors.

The show gives feet to William Shakespeare's claim that all the world's a stage.

There's nothing secret about Truman's life—not a single breath, not a single move. Unaware that he's continually in the spotlight, he lives in the straightjacket of control and subconscious manipulation to feed the ego of Cristof and the curiosity of the worldwide audience. That is, until his late twenties when he begins noticing unusual events in his life that simply cannot be misconstrued as mere coincidences. He wakes up to the delusion that has consumed his life and moves toward truth—a greater reality.

When Truman tries to escape the island by sailboat, he encounters a violent, man-made storm ordered by Cristof. It's an attempt to terrify Truman and hinder him from leaving and ruining the show. After surviving the hellish storm, the clouds part. The sun shines. He sails toward calmer, deeper waters until the bow strikes and rips through the backdrop of the set.

In a heart-wrenching moment, as tears fall, he punches the backdrop, steps out of the boat, walks along a ramp and up a staircase to what appears to be an exit door. His inner man is fully awakened, and his suspicions are confirmed. His whole life has been a charade.

Looking through the lens of Truman's life can be beneficial for women who are in the wilderness after abortion. Undoubtedly, we, too, cross paths with people who awaken us to truth. We encounter information and events designed to inspire us to believe we are not as invaluable or disconnected as we feel. We need to be reminded that the storm *is* going to break, the sun is *still* shining, and everything is going to be *alright*. We also need encouragement and reassurance that even though we may feel alone and isolated, there is a group of people cheering for us, rooting for us, supporting us, and maybe even praying for us to step out of the boat, find the exit door, and walk into freedom.

During his life, Truman is approached by a small number of genuinely concerned people who try to warn him that his reality is false. One woman pleads with him to believe his world is a lie: "Everybody knows about it. Everybody knows everything you do. They're pretending."[2] As his suspicions of a reality beyond his fabricated life increase, actors are sent to maintain the illusion and persuade him to believe everything is fine. The further he moves toward truth, the more resistance he faces. The TV show can only function and continue as long as Truman buys into this false reality. In other words, keeping him in a cage is paramount to the show's success.

When those who have experienced abortion examine new ideas or heed the voices and people who are *for* us—though they may not be perched on the loudest, most prominent platforms—we can move toward a truth that promises to liberate us. Like Truman, we may face obstacles. Their intensity may even increase. Rest assured, though, that a positive outcome exists if we, like Truman, acknowledge our suspicions, fight the fear of resistance and discovery, and begin to search for a solution to our problem. Marcus Aurelius beckons us to advance: "If someone is able to show me that what I think or do is not right, I will happily change, for I seek the truth, by which no one was ever truly harmed. It is the person who continues in his self-deception and ignorance who is harmed."[3]

The resistance to Truman's quest for reality rains down from the outside. Figuratively speaking, a majority of people in his fabricated world perpetuate the lie of his unreality. Literally speaking, Cristof sends not one but two major weather events to defeat Truman. The first brings torrential rain and wind. The second brings powerful forked lightning and massive waves—whatever it takes to pummel or capsize Truman's will and determination to get to the truth.

We, too, face storms of resistance. The external opposition is the continued, disheartening denial of the harm caused by abortion. We long for freedom but doubt there's anyone who can guide us through darkness into daylight. The inner straightjacket of control and manipulation within our subconscious realm is stealthier. We remain oblivious, or we convince ourselves that "that day" is not affecting our lives.

Like the tiniest pebble in a sneaker, however, we feel the rub. Our brains record the annoyance, but they also run interference so we don't suspect anything or question what's happening inside. We sense something is wrong, but after months or decades of avoidance, we're unable to pinpoint the cause or reason.

Theresa Burke offers this wisdom: "One cannot simply practice stuffing techniques and push the memory into oblivion. The path to healing is not found in going through the motions, trying hard *not* to feel, hiding one's emotions, or convincing oneself that a mistaken choice was good. Memories *will* surface."[4]

In other words, time doesn't heal all wounds. Especially this one.

Frederick Buechner observes, "We never really forget anything, they say, and all our pasts lie fathoms deep in us somewhere waiting for some stray sight or smell or scrap of sound to bring them to the surface again."[5]

Our abortion may not resurrect in the months following our experience or even two or twenty years later. But eventually, it will arrive at our breakfast table.[6] It is a guarantee that at some point, near or far, all things that have been hidden will be revealed. Anything secret will become known and come to light.[7] It's not a matter of *if*, but *when* it will stare us in the face.

Dr. Miriam Grossman illuminates the significance of this reality: "A soldier may survive the battlefield and initially appear to cope well. Only later—maybe years later—may he begin to dwell on what happened, to obsess and dream about it. ... As a person ages, earlier traumas will be examined and appraised from a new angle, depending on subsequent events: marriages, divorces, births, miscarriages, infertility, menopause, loss of loved ones."[8]

Because there's little discussion of how to heal the ache and heartbreak of abortion, we settle. We conform to silence. We sit in defeat, assuming no one can help us—that nothing about the past can be reversed or undone. Kim Ketola describes the effect of these kinds of thoughts:

> Those kinds of thoughts can be paralyzing. That's not some fatal flaw in you. It's natural, normal. The law of inertia says an object in a state of motion (or rest) tends to remain in that state until an external force is applied. Gravity forces an object to fall and momentum makes it move. Abortion can put you in a spiritual inertia—feeling stuck, depressed, numb, unable to befriend or love with any intimacy. You feel … helpless and immobilized.[9]

Silence is mistaken for resilience. Theresa Burke explains the silence this way: "Abortion is a deeply private and complex experience. For most women, their feelings and memories about an abortion simply do not lend themselves to casual conversation. Women who will enthusiastically compare pregnancy and delivery stories over tea would never dream of talking about their feelings and memories related to past abortions."[10]

Pat Layton is another courageous woman with support at the ready. She knows first-hand the devastation of abortion and acknowledges that we carry heavy burdens and suffer severe consequences when we hide the secret of abortion deep in our hearts. In her book *Surrendering the Secret,* she encourages greater openness:

> As post-abortive women, the thought of being "exposed" or "found out" terrifies us. Most likely, fear of exposure of the pregnancy was a factor in choosing abortion in the first place. That's one reason why many women have guarded their secret for years. But consider this: Whom do we really protect by holding onto the secret? We're covering up the deceiver's lie that abortion doesn't hurt women and are reinforcing society's belief that we are unaffected by the choice. Remaining silent keeps us in the darkness of the lie, but freedom comes in exposing it.[11]

Dr. Julius Fogel, an obstetrician and psychiatrist who personally performed over twenty thousand abortions, is an unlikely person and professional to counter the narrative that "mostly people are extremely resilient." In a Washington Post article, *The Real Anguish of Abortions*, he validates what many of us know:

> There is no question about the emotional grief and mourning following an abortion. It shows up in various forms. I've had patients who had abortions a year or two ago—women who did the best thing at the time for themselves—but it still bothers them. Many come in—some are just mute, some hostile. Some burst out crying. ... There is no question in my mind that we are disturbing a life process.[12]

His comments reaffirm an interview he had with the same journalist prior to the 1973 Roe v. Wade decision:

> Every woman—whatever her age, background, or sexuality—has a trauma at destroying a pregnancy. A level of humanness is touched. This is a part of her own life. When she destroys a pregnancy, she is destroying herself. There is no way it can be innocuous. One is dealing with the life force. It is totally beside the point whether or not you think a life is there. You cannot deny that something is being created and that this creation is physically happening. ... Often the trauma may sink into the unconscious and never surface in the woman's lifetime. But it is not as harmless and casual an event as many in the pro-abortion crowd insist. A psychological price is paid. It may be alienation; it may be a pushing away from human warmth, perhaps a hardening of the maternal instinct. Something happens on the deeper levels of a woman's consciousness when she destroys a pregnancy. I know that as a psychiatrist.[13]

There is good news for us. We're not alone. There is an army of sincere, loving people who are willing to come alongside us to help us in our time of need. They know, to use the words of Dr. Seuss, we've been left in the lurch and cannot cure or heal ourselves of all the bang-ups and hang-ups. That we've come down from the lurch with an unpleasant bump. That we're all in a slump, and un-slumping ourselves is not easily done.[14]

They know the way out.

They choose *not* to ignore or gloss over the struggles we face. Nor do they offer trite solutions. With great empathy, they concur with Dr. Dan Allender who says, "A problem cannot be substantially resolved until it is honestly faced."[15] They acknowledge what many of us know in our hearts—that we have done something terribly wrong. They affirm what Max Lucado says in *Anxious for Nothing*, "There is a guilt that sits in the soul like a concrete block."[16] They're willing to address our wounds and dis-ease with honesty—as few mental health experts, medical professionals, and hard-hat religious people do.

They don't point fingers at us or heap condemnation on us. They're not the self-satisfied type who look down their noses in a comparative kind of way and say, "Well, I haven't murdered anyone." On the contrary, they know the reality of our emotional tug-of-war. Like Truman's sincere friends, their goal is not to persuade us that everything is fine but to validate that our failure, shame, confusion, disturbances, and despair are not symptoms of being crazy. They long to help us cast off the weight of guilt and its accompanying inner turmoil to lead us with compassion and love to a highway of hope and a pathway to freedom. Truly, their heart motive is to help us awaken to a greater reality—something we can't fathom.

I can relate to Truman. My wake-up call came in my late twenties.

After college and after my relationship with the big fish boyfriend ended, I gave myself a pep talk. It was necessary, for my sense of inner peace, to surrender the worry of what might happen if he failed to protect our secret. I reminded myself neither of us had broached the subject since "that day" and concluded all would be well. I wanted to work to become the best version of myself and to secure my self-worth. Appearing to have it all together—at least on the outside—was essential. "Impostors," says Brennan Manning, "always prefer appearances to reality. Rationalization begins with a look in the mirror. We don't like the sight of ourselves as we really are, so we try cosmetics, makeup, the right light, and the proper accessories to develop an acceptable image of ourselves. We rely on the stylish disguise that has made us look good or at least look away from our true selves. Self-deception mortgages our sinfulness and prevents us from seeing ourselves as we really are. Ragamuffins."[17]

I didn't date anyone exclusively and for the next several years worked, volunteered in the community, traveled, and focused on self-improvement. I also went to church with my family, albeit irregularly. To my great surprise, Sarah and I reconciled our friendship during this time. We picked up where we had left off, like we hadn't skipped a beat.

In a fortunate spark of serendipity, I met my Prince Charming. We were married within a year and a half.

Two and a half years later, we were thrilled to learn I was pregnant. Excitement filled our home. That is until I had my first visit with the obstetrician. That's when I felt the first sizable shift—like a movement of tectonic plates in my soul. While completing the new patient documentation, I was confronted with questions about abortion. Had I ever had one? If so, how many? And when? I paused. *Uh oh. Abortion? Why am I dealing with this again? How many? Repeat abortions? Does anyone have more than one? How does she survive?*

I hadn't thought about "that day" for years. Suddenly I was transported back in time. I found myself, as The Pretenders sing, "back on the chain gang."[18] Shame hovered. Thoughts raced. *Isn't that in my past? How humiliating. And despicable. Do I have to be honest? How can I be? I will never disclose that decision. That was then, and this is now. No one ever needs to know. For that matter, who and why would anyone need that information?* I emphatically checked the box "NO" and quickly addressed the remaining questions before being called in to see the doctor.

The appointment brought devastating news. No heartbeat. The doctor offered words of compassion and mentioned miscarriage happens more than we realize. She suggested we wait a few months before trying to conceive. Prince Charming and I drove home and agreed that despite our hopes and spirits being dashed, we would aim to keep a positive outlook. We admitted our sorrow, conceded the possibility that the baby hadn't been developing normally, and assured each other that mercy had prevailed. This seemed to bring the most comfort—for a short while anyway.

Admittedly, I struggled to find closure. For weeks, I quietly juggled the possibilities behind the "why" of having to experience such a painful loss. I pondered the truth that all of life is filled with mystery. And just as I resolved to let go of the need for an answer, a piercing sting of accusing arrows penetrated my heart: *You know this is punishment for what you did. You deserve it. You should have never done what you did.* Rehearsing the thoughts knocked any remaining wind out of my sail. *Perhaps I* am *being punished. Perhaps I* do *deserve this pain.* Dazed and confused, I gave the ole grin-and-bear-it strategy a dusting, exhaled, and stood firm. *Push through. Be strong. Get through it. Keep going.*

Life marched on.

Surprise! Eleven months later, we welcomed our first child.

The wonder of pregnancy, our son's entrance into this world, and the joy he brought to us and to our families hugged my heart. I couldn't help but entertain the idea that his life and motherhood were signs, if not proof, that I wasn't being punished after all. I remember feeling wholeheartedly confident I was the recipient of the kindness of the cosmos. I sincerely believed our son was given to us as a gift—so much so that the name we gave him means gift of God. He was the baby I didn't deserve. I was grateful and flying high.

Within a year, I had a second miscarriage. I was emotionally knocked down but not destroyed. Familiar accusations roared, and the idea of divine discipline resurfaced. This time, however, none of it made sense to me. It was on the heels of losing this baby that I began to feel a restlessness, a stirring—an internal burden—to re-examine my high school decision. The majority of memories were stuffed far down and submerged, like a well clogged with sediment and dirt. But I wondered, *What exactly happens in these clinics? What actually happened that day?*

Late one night, while fighting a barrage of conflicting emotions, disappointment, and fear of discovering what I had done "that day," I walked downstairs to the computer, sat in a chair at the desk, took a deep breath, placed my fingers on the keyboard, and slowly typed a-b-o-r-t-i-o-n in the search bar. I couldn't have imagined I would enter into a world of information that shocked, rocked, and disturbed me to the core. Suffice it to say, there was no shortage of detailed articles or disturbing, gruesome images. Hours later, I closed my eyes in anguish over what I read and saw. Tears streamed down my cheeks. I remember saying out loud, *"What? I did that? I ended the life of a little person? Oh, no. I could never and will never do that again. And I could never support such evil."*

Again, life continued on.

Ten months later, we welcomed our second child. A daughter. And three years after her arrival, we welcomed another son.

Around this time, our nation was gearing up for a presidential election. I began to notice an avalanche of conversation on the topic of abortion. Pro. Anti. For. Against. Support. Opposition. Women. Men. Religious people. Non-religious people. Opinions, commentary, and arguments abounded on all sides. It made my head spin.

To me, it seemed like a groundswell of sentiments had suddenly overtaken the country. But I was wrong. *Very* wrong. The cultural battle surrounding abortion was not sudden; it had been raging front and center for decades. I was just a bona fide latecomer to the debate.

My eyes and my mind were only beginning to open to the enormity of the subject. Internet research was new to me as was the storehouse of information. I became immersed in every aspect of the topic: the history of abortion in the U.S. and abroad, prominent names linked to it, its terminology, court rulings, procedure descriptions, images, abortion providers, numbers, statistics, pregnancy resource centers, articles, public policy positions, and the whole spectrum of viewpoints.

In the privacy of our family room, I began digging my way out of ignorance and uncovering the dizzying deception of abortion! My boat was on course to pierce the thin veil of lies, and soon, reality would come crashing in.

A REFLECTION

Ann Patchett, author of What Now? *offers hope and inspiration for anyone at a crossroads: " 'What now' is not just a panic-stricken question tossed out into a dark unknown. 'What now' can also be our joy. It is a declaration of possibility, of promise, of chance. It acknowledges that our future is open, that we may well do more than anyone expected of us, that at every point in our development we are still striving to grow. ... But there is another time, a better time, when we see our lives as a series of choices, and 'What now' represents our excitement and our future, the very vitality of life. It's up to you to choose a life that will keep expanding."*[19]

P.S. You really are loved.

SEVEN

Running Away

Hope begins in the dark,
the stubborn hope that if you just show up and
try to do the right thing,
the dawn will come.
You wait and watch and work:
you don't give up.
—Anne Lamott—

THE MOVIEGOER'S BINX BOLLING SAYS, "THE SEARCH IS WHAT anyone would undertake if he were not sunk in the everydayness of his own life. … To become aware of the possibility of the search is to be onto something. Not to be onto something is to be in despair."[1] In the season of raising young, vibrant children, I was privately ensconced in the search. A fact-finding mission about abortion and its associated cultural concerns was my quiet side gig. Such a pursuit hardly qualifies anyone for a popularity contest or keynote speaking engagement, but I wasn't interested in or fastened to the mundane, much less "everydayness." I was onto something.

Why, you might ask, do soldiers willingly return to the battleground of their worst nightmares? Why would anyone want to fritter away her free time on the topic of abortion? Well, for starters, I was baffled by how and why our culture embraces the idea that the procedure somehow leads to freedom. Important and valid questions deserving honest, principled answers surfaced. *Why, if the United States averages a million abortions each year, do women feel so alone? Where is this sisterhood of millions of women? Why, despite having loving family and friends, do we feel so isolated—like it's us against the world? Why, whether for days or decades, do we continue to wander and feel so forsaken? Is our emotional restlessness really an anomaly or a freak exception? When or how can we ever be free of the heavy baggage of shame and stigma? Does anybody care?*

I was becoming increasingly convinced that abortion, though peddled as a quick, easy, freedom-generating remedy for unintended pregnancies, is nothing but an illusion leading to heartache, pain, and misery—in body, soul, and spirit. Women, to borrow Chuck Colson's words, "cannot see how their liberty has enslaved them to alienation, betrayal, loneliness, and inhumanity. They have grown so accustomed to the dark, they don't even realize the lights are out."[2] Somehow— some way—someone flipped the light switch for me. I was searching for answers. For a way up and out. Everything in me was beginning to oppose abortion.

The big-picture question was what to do and how to move forward with the knowledge I had. It's also a question for you if you find yourself softening as you learn and process new information about abortion. Peterson encourages us, "This very strangeness can open up new reality to us. An accident, a tragedy, a disaster of any kind [or waking up to the truth of abortion] can force the realization that the world is not predictable, that reality is far more extensive than our habitual perception of it. With the pain and in the midst of alienation a sense of freedom can occur."[3]

It was a season of discovery with its own twists and turns. My story was like Dr. Seuss's Schlottz—"the Crumple-horned, Web-footed,

Green-bearded Schlottz whose tail is entailed with unsolvable knots."[4] On one hand, while resigned to the fact I could never rewrite my history, I yearned for an unraveling of all the tangled emotional mess. Ripples of frustration, distress, and self-disappointment resurfaced as did every imaginable shoulda, coulda, woulda. Newfound emotions emerged too. I faced waves of feeling tricked, cheated, and betrayed. I felt exploited as I read and analyzed rarely-mentioned books, articles, and studies exposing the secrecy and web of deceit surrounding the abortion industry and illuminating decades of evidence of how it's marketed, sold, and reported. Testimonies of nurses, physicians, and administrators who changed their minds and stopped performing or facilitating the procedure captured my attention.

Dr. Bernard Nathanson, for example, was an obstetrician who admitted to knowing the abortion issue as no one else had. In the late 1960s, he was one of the three founders of the National Abortion Rights Action League who worked hard to take abortion from its infancy to being legal, affordable, and available on demand—the "unimaginably gargantuan monster" it is today. As an abortion doctor, he claimed seventy-five thousand encounters with abortion. He personally performed five thousand and presided over seventy thousand.[5] In a great reversal, disregarding such staggering credentials, he changed his mind on abortion. He credits his awakening to the 1973 introduction and rise of the (then) new technologies that gave him a window into the womb—fetal heart monitoring, real-time ultrasound, and fetoscopy to name three. He said, "As a result of all this technology … looking at the baby … I finally came to the conviction that this was my patient. This was a person! … This was purely a change of mind as a result of this fantastic technology and new insights and perceptions I had into the nature of the unborn child."[6]

He carried a deep sense of responsibility and a profound burden for his past and part in ushering in what he called the barbaric age. The irony of ironies is that after his awakening and before his death in 2011, he was committed to writing books and articles, creating films, and giving interviews about abortion. He gave open and honest public talks and shared the sobering account of his journey to renouncing his commitment to abortion in his very moving autobiography, *The Hand of God.*

Carol Everett owned and operated two abortion clinics in Texas, and her memoir *Blood Money* tells her story of walking away and leaving behind a very lucrative, for-profit business. In one interview, she describes with disarming candor her personal experience and close perspective on what she calls the largest, uncontrolled industry in the nation: "Women don't choose abortion. Women are sold an abortion at a very crisis time in their lives as the simple, easy answer. It is not a choice women make. It's a marketed product."[7]

The most surprising truths I unearthed during my research appear in *Won by Love,* the story of Norma McCorvey. They might shock you, too. Norma is the "Jane Roe" of *Roe v. Wade.* Though she played a pivotal role in legalizing abortion, she admits she never had one. Not a single one! And she was never raped. Although she claimed to have been raped in order to gain public support for abortion, she later admitted it was all a lie. Lawyers affiliated with the case, the ones who based the entire case on the rape that never happened, had had abortions, but Norma placed each of her three children for adoption. After fighting for and helping to win the right to secure an abortion and spending decades working in clinics, she shocked the world when she changed her mind and rescinded all support for it. It was said at the time, "The poster child for abortion jumped off the poster."[8]

I was acutely sensitive to the stories of ordinary, courageous women who chose to go public with their abortion histories and regrets. There is no shortage of personal accounts. I couldn't have imagined being so raw and fearless. Still, they opened my eyes to the probability that I was surrounded by women who were equally silent about their abortion experience, not to mention plenty of others with strong but private pro-life convictions.

On the other hand, because I was delving into a subject far outside everyday, ordinary conversation, I found myself knee-deep in yet another kind of alienation. Since the "A" word is so emotionally charged and rankles most everyone, I felt no freedom to unload my knowledge on fellow travelers, even politely. Moms at school, at swim lessons, in the neighborhood, and at beach gatherings, along with my entire family (except my husband) would have looked at me wide-eyed and uttered an exasperated snort or blurted out the famous Arnold Jackson line, "Whatcha talkin' bout, Willis?"

Most people are grateful to be left out of such conversations. I desperately wanted to speak, but broaching the subject was too daunting. As Theresa Burke says, "The general public has very little understanding of the post-abortion experience. ... There is very little social awareness of the need to support women ... after an abortion."[9] I was unwilling to risk being deemed impolite or dismissed as a crackpot. Exposing myself was out of the question. The very thought of being shunned, snubbed, or ostracized undid me.

The twists and turns led me to an impasse. My values were shifting and transforming at warp speed. A strong desire for justice was taking up residence in my thought life. I was growing increasingly concerned for girls and young women contemplating abortion who had no notion of the possible scenarios and severity of problems that lie ahead. But I was in uncharted waters. I was conflicted about how to freely discuss abortion while pretending I had never had one. Despite the dilemma, an undercurrent of peace seemed to quiet my lingering inner confusion and gently prod me forward on what felt like a peculiar treasure hunt.

Coincidentally, Prince Charming and I began to attend the church where our children were in preschool. To my great surprise, I met several sincere people who were passionate about and willing to address the verboten topic of abortion. They were kind, compassionate, and loving—qualities that certainly didn't square with how abortion opponents were characterized in the media or political world. They weren't radical. They didn't speak with an air of superiority or condemnation. Nor did they offer flippant comments like, "Women who have had abortions are horrible people." I felt safe in their presence and was eager to listen to their opinions, ask questions about discoveries I had uncovered, and learn from them. In the words of

Brennan Manning, "Something powerful had quickened me out of the sluggishness of everyday life and into an active search for what life is really about."[10]

The best and most beautiful part of this season of life was that as I was accumulating and expanding my knowledge, my heart was softening. My convictions were forming, and my courage was building, too. It was becoming increasingly difficult *not* to share. I saw no point in being a passive collector of information. I was like a broker —motivated to initiate discussions to educate people and willing to trade what I knew.[11] To do *nothing* with the material would mean ignoring my internal wiring and the strong desire that had taken hold within me. My life felt like an arrow, drawn back on the bowstring of an archer's bow, ready to fly.

There was just one thing standing in the way—the proverbial elephant in the living room—my past.

Michelle McClain-Walters expounds, "Many times when we feel the pull of destiny, we also feel the pull of the past. ... Fear creeps in causing us to believe that if we move forward, somehow things we have done in the past will come back to sabotage our future."[12] My personal history with abortion was a deeply anchored secret, and I was bound and determined to keep it that way—even with Prince Charming. Shame and fear form a forcefield that holds power over its victims. Thankfully, a consuming curiosity compelled me to press on, so much so that I acted on a friend's recommendation and joined a group of women whose objective is to educate legislators on cultural issues. This was an opportunity to make a difference by contributing and sharing my knowledge, passion, and female point of view with those writing and passing legislation.

My rationale for working in the public policy arena was to make a difference for good. However, the desire was more deeply rooted in the subconscious idea that I could somehow right my course or offset the wrongs of my past by participating in, promoting, and advancing a more noble and virtuous cause. I reasoned, arrogantly perhaps, that looking normal and doing good might help me earn my way back into the good grace of God, score points, or somehow balance the scales. In

Post Abortion Trauma, Jeanette Vought discusses a range of immediate and repressed emotional effects of abortion. I had experienced depression, shame, guilt, grief, denial, and anger, but the rise of what she calls "bargaining" was brand new. With pinpoint accuracy, she describes the driving motive: "Post-abortive women bargain or try to make amends for their abortion by becoming active in the pro-life movement or a crisis pregnancy ministry. ... If she has not dealt with her grief, she is only trying to make up for what she has done."[13]

Regardless of any underlying or latent reasons, I met gracious, action-oriented women seasoned in government advocacy work. They welcomed me with enthusiasm and unselfishly imparted wisdom. My knowledge of civics had come from textbooks and teachers. This new, vibrant, and practical learning period enriched my understanding of how to be a citizen in a government of, by, and for the people. I learned that my voice matters. The influence of the intellect, humility, and authenticity of this group of women ignited my interest to be more public in matters of life and liberty. Some willingly shared their backstories and how they overcame incredible odds to be able to stand shoulder-to-shoulder with elected leaders. I was encouraged by their ability to speak truth to power about important issues with grace, empathy, and tenderness.

What fascinated me most, though, was their inner beauty. They radiated hopefulness and optimism for a brighter future. They often prayed for one another, for the success of their efforts, for the American citizenry, and for our nation. Their prayers were unlike anything I had experienced in my upbringing and frequently brought tears to my eyes. What's more, these women sounded as if they had a certain, transparent, and intimate connection with God—as if He heard their prayers. And the irony of it all? As broken and raggamuffin-like as I was on the inside, I was drawn to them. To their cause. To their goal of educating others. To whoever their God was.

I would have given anything to be like them, to be one of them. My admiration for them ran deep and wide. My heart longed to belong. I was eager to learn and work alongside these women who exuded leadership, goodwill, and love. Despite the inner cowering, clamoring, and reticence, I dove in head first.

After a several-year stint in the public policy arena, I discerned a change of seasons. The time required to lobby and stay connected with the network of women was ramping up. So were the demands of my family. I felt physically and emotionally tired. Even though I had a strong interest in advocacy, devotion to my family was my top priority. Sacrificing it by not being present or in the moment with them wasn't an option, so Prince Charming and I agreed that the best course was to focus on my most valued work—family life. Truthfully, a significant contributing factor to the fatigue was the lurking stress and mounting inner pressure to mirror what I loved most about these friends—their virtue and goodness.

It was a self-imposed, impossible climb. And I was the chief poser. I didn't have an adequate supply of spiritual cosmetics or light in my personal arsenal to continue the masquerade. Brennan Manning shines a spotlight on people like me as those "trying to fix themselves, improve their prayer life, make themselves presentable to God and lovable to others. Sooner rather than later, they're appalled by their inconsistency, dejected by their mediocrity, and depressed because they haven't met their own lofty expectations. In the self-help spiritual swamp, there are no survivors."[14]

The condescending, condemning, and accusing voice in my head returned with ferocity. *You can't continue with these people. You're a fraud. A hypocrite. You're not one of them. Why do you think you can hide your past from them? What will happen when they discover the real you—you, the one who took the life of her child? They will shun you and cast you out. No one likes a hypocrite.*

Alas, the weight of carrying my secret with its attendant shame, the humiliating burden of pretense, and the fear of looking foolish was too heavy. Too draining. Freedom was too elusive. I couldn't continue to move forward with all my falsity, baggage, and brokenness. Brené Brown describes this struggle:

> The stories of our struggles are difficult for everyone to own, and if we have worked hard to make sure everything looks just right on the outside, the stakes are high when it comes to truth-telling. This is why shame loves perfectionists. It's so easy to keep us quiet. In addition to the fear of disappointing people or pushing them away with our stories, we're also afraid that if we tell our stories, the weight of a single experience will collapse upon us. There is a real fear that we can be buried or defined by an experience that, in reality, is only a sliver of who we are.[15]

I decided to do what any overwhelmed, bedraggled soldier would do. I did an about-face, marched off the field in defeat, and mailed a resignation letter. Then I ran. I ran away. I ran away as abruptly as I had arrived in their midst, utterly convinced I could never qualify or measure up to anyone's expectations—whether perceived or actual.

It's been said that running away from problems is a race that can never be won. One of my elementary school teachers once told the class that running away from problems is like trying to lose your shadow. In my case, both expressions rang true. I couldn't run faster than my thoughts or escape my shadow. Little did I know I was on a collision course with not only *what* I was running from but also *Whom*.

Within weeks, two things happened that were as mystifying to me as Truman's encounter with the production light falling from the vaulted sky. They were bolts from the blue. First, I received a large manila envelope in the mailbox. To this day, I don't know who sent it; there was no return address. Inside was a twelve-page newspaper insert. Its three-inch banner headline announcing "HOPE AND HEALING" seized my attention. Words in the publication's lead paragraph like *past abortion, joy, gratitude, compassion, and mercy* jumped off the paper. Initially, I was alarmed. My heart raced. I looked outward and gazed upward. *Who sees me? Who sent me this publication? How does anyone know?*

Other words, including *millions, suffer in silence, overcoming unresolved grief, aching hearts* and *secret pain,* also appeared on the front page. The final paragraph read, "This publication is for anyone who has ever been directly or indirectly affected by abortion—and that includes nearly all of us. When you read these pages with an open heart and mind, you will learn the secrets of hope and healing that can directly benefit you or your loved ones."[16] Hope? Unresolved grief? Complete healing? I had never seen or heard these words attached to the "A" word. This was a first. I was onto something!

The other thing that happened was that out of nowhere came a telephone call from a mere acquaintance. It catapulted me into three weeks of frenzied activity—the search of all searches. I credit this arrangement as the divine lifeline that lassoed me back into the treasure hunt and pointed me to *the* defining moment of my life. The details, so intricately and colorfully woven together, serve to demonstrate that my story isn't a cleverly invented narrative. It's simply impossible to have imagined or written them into the chronicle of my life.

Gail's call rang through on a Monday morning that winter. After an exchange of pleasantries, she asked if I had received an invitation (mailed weeks earlier) to a gathering she was hosting in her home that Thursday evening. Initially, I felt flattered; however, I was caught off guard for two reasons. First, I hadn't received the invitation. Second, I scarcely knew her—our children, though different ages, knew each other from school and the swim team. I replied that I had not. Then came her verbal invitation. She was a board member of the local affiliate of a large, national abortion provider and asked me to attend a fundraiser at her home.

After she asked if I would be interested in joining her and her group, a hush descended. I stared at the phone, slack-jawed with disbelief and frozen in surprise. *This battle isn't behind me. Fundraiser for abortion? What kind of mark do I have on my forehead to indicate to anyone that I would donate one penny to an abortion provider?*

Silence from my end continued as I fished for anything more intelligible than the babble and gibberish sitting on the tip of my tongue. *What am I going to tell this woman?* My heart hurt for her. I wondered if, like me, she'd had an abortion. Seconds seemed like minutes.

One might credit the matter to blind chance or dumb luck, but I had the distinct impression there was something far greater and grander going on than just a random invitation or conversation. I had been hit with a headwind. Wavering between opinions was no longer my option. This wasn't about Gail. It wasn't about her invitation. It wasn't about the fundraiser or the abortion provider. There was no mistaking that this was a climactic showdown, a moment of truth. I was being served a redo on a silver platter. The opportunity to confidently take a stand. To choose. I was experiencing the chance—in a life-opening and redemptive sort of way—to revisit the choice I made years earlier when my friend Sarah asked me over the phone, "What are you going to do?"

Before I was able to say a single word, Gail spoke. She apologized for assuming I was pro-choice (her words) and for offending me. With a smile on my face, I assured her she hadn't offended me. I mentioned I could possibly attend the event at her home but needed to check the family schedule before making a decision. I asked her, out of curiosity, how my name surfaced on her radar. She shared that she had taken my name and number from the directory of our former church. She casually mentioned the pastor's involvement with her group and in the same breath tried to persuade me I could be religious and pro-choice. Gulp! I was quietly confident her assertion didn't ring true. I simply told her I'd call her the next day.

That night, before falling asleep, I had my first-ever conscious conversation with God. As Prince Charming lay sleeping, I looked toward heaven and said, "God, I don't know why this happened to me today. And I don't know why Gail believes someone can be religious *and* support abortion. I need You to tell me if I'm supposed to be part of the event at her house. I'm willing to go to learn, but if You don't want others to think I support abortion, I won't go. I need to hear from You. I need Your answer."

Hours later, shortly after 2:00 a.m., I was jolted awake by a gentle voice that said, "Don't go." Ears and eyes wide open, I knew in an instant the voice didn't belong to Prince Charming. Nor was this a dream. This voice was unique. Pleasant. Lovingly firm. I lay there, silent and motionless. The two-syllable answer was everything I needed. Then, something far greater than my intuition suggested inviting Gail to lunch to explain why being religious and supporting abortion are mutually exclusive, like heads or tails. The only way I can describe the experience is to tell you I had an inner knowing—deep on the inside. Before my head could understand or comprehend it and before I could reason it out, I knew in my knower that I had been given an assignment. A directive.

The title of Anne Lamott's book sums up what happened that night: *Help, Thanks, Wow: The Three Essential Prayers.* God had certainly wowed me. By morning, I felt fearless. I knew running away—even for one more day—was an exercise in utter futility. There was nowhere else to run. I had been given marching orders, and I had a lot of research and studying ahead of me if Gail agreed to meet. Nadia Comaneci once said, "I don't run away from a challenge because I'm afraid. Instead, I run toward it because the only way to escape fear is to trample it beneath your feet."[17]

I planned to call Gail to decline her invitation and invite her to lunch, but, to my surprise, she called me soon after the children left for school. She apologized again for offending me, and we had a polite conversation. I summoned the courage to ask her to lunch, and she accepted. We arranged to meet three weeks later. When the call ended, I immediately phoned a friend and asked her to send me every bit of information she had about the abortion provider, including its history, statistics, income, and presence in the U.S. and around the globe. In the words of Ann Brashares, I couldn't erase the past. I couldn't even change it. But I believed wholeheartedly God was offering me the opportunity to make it right.[18]

A REFLECTION

Michelle McClain-Walters inspires us to realize that our broken dreams and broken lives can become the greatest source of hope. We have a destiny to chase. When we resist staying where we are and choose instead to step into the unknown and venture past limitations and boundaries—either self-imposed or imposed by the culture—we can discover a life of fulfillment. If you are settling for the status quo, you are already disqualified. Stretching involves change. Stretching sets you apart from others. Stretching gives you a shot at significance. Let God stretch you. Like a rubber band, God will stretch you and give you the capacity for more. God is the only one who can stretch you and not break you.[19]

P.S. You are loved.

EIGHT

The Whisper

They have known the counterfeit so strongly
And for so long and so deeply
That when they're set free,
They know the truth in a way you cannot.
—Unknown—

IN HIS CLASSIC BESTSELLER, *THE RAGAMUFFIN GOSPEL*, BRENNAN Manning paints a brilliant picture of those gathered in heaven. With a refreshing blend of compassion and boldness, he includes a woman rescued from the battlefield. "I believe that among the countless number of people standing in front of the throne … I shall see the woman who had an abortion and is haunted by guilt and remorse but did the best she could faced with grueling alternatives."[1]

Outrageous. Scandalous. Unprecedented. You wonder, "How can this be?"

He continues, "She's part of a multitude who at times got defeated, soiled by life, and bested by trials, wearing the bloodied garments of life's tribulations, but through it all clung to the faith."[2]

Good news like this might puzzle you. Perhaps it excites and encourages you. On the other hand, big, mysterious words like heaven and faith might tempt you to shrink back. But please don't. For goodness' sake, you've come too far to give up or go under. We're survivors, you and I. You're like Truman in the storm scene—refusing to quit, fighting to stay alive, conquering the raging tempest ordered by the antagonist. Like him, you're on to something! Stand strong. Ignore the doubt, discouragement, and inner and outer turmoil. Resist the strident voice in your head, rationalizations, and the mind tricks of self-commentary.

Do you perceive you're in a contest far beyond and far more consequential than what you see and feel in the physical world? Will you determine to see it through? Let's be as resolute as Truman when he leans backward in the midst of the storm, lifts his face toward the dome, and shouts upward, "Is that the best you can do? You're gonna have to kill me!"[3] His battle—like mine, like yours, like ours—is for the highest stake. Victory of good over evil awaits you. Freedom over oppression, shame, manipulation, and control awaits you. Run headlong. Remember, life is a continuous exploration of ever more reality, a constant battle against everyone and anything that corrupts or diminishes it.[4]

Let's pick up where we left off with *The Truman Show* so I can draw parallels between the movie's final scene and my collision course with Gail. In what I call the freedom scene, after Truman's sailboat pierces the movie set backdrop and brings the boat to an abrupt halt, he walks from the sailboat to a staircase. He climbs to the top, sees a single door marked "exit," and pushes the door open. From somewhere unknown, Christof, the show's creator and chief oppressor and villain, speaks his name. A startled Truman whips around.

Their ensuing dialogue illuminates the cosmic battle raging in each of our lives. The lesser force—always deceiving, conniving, malevolent—aims to tighten the shackles and chains, stir up fear, and perpetuate the enslavement of those held captive on the battlefield. By contrast, a strength and a wisdom—invisible and always greater—work benevolently behind the scenes. Ever pursuing and always wooing the *true man*—in our case, the *true woman*—love aims to free the captive and release her into a life of hope, destiny, strength, and purpose. Let's listen in:

> "Truman. You can speak. We can hear you."
> "Who are you?"
> "I'm the creator of a television show that gives hope, joy, and inspiration to millions."
> "Then who am I?"
> "You're the star."
> With a look of "not believing it," Truman asks, "Was nothing real?"
> "You were real. It's what made you so good to watch."

Truman turns toward the exit door.

> "Listen to me, Truman. There's no more truth out there than there is in the world I created for you. The same lies. The same deceit. But in my world, you have nothing to fear. I know you better than you know yourself."
> "I never had a camera in my head," says Truman as he stares into the doorway.
> "You're afraid. That's why you can't leave."

Truman wobbles between staying and going.

> "It's okay, Truman. I understand. I have been watching you your whole life. I was watching when you were born. I was watching when you took your first step. I watched you on your first day of school. Hehe—the episode when you lost your first tooth. Hehe—you can't leave Truman. You belong here. With

me. Talk to me. Say something. You're on television. You're live to the whole world."

Truman responds decisively.

"In case I don't see ya, good afternoon, good evening, and good night."

He chuckles, bows, stands, stretches his arms wide, turns, and, with the entire world (the viewing audience) cheering him on, Truman confidently walks through the doorway into a greater reality. Exit stage left![5]

Gail's phone call was the gift that pierced the shadow of reality for me. It abruptly halted my life, pointed me to the proverbial exit door atop the stairs, and led me to true living. As I would soon discover, the significance of the scenario—a veritable stair climb—was anything but ordinary.

I don't remember much of daily life while in the throes of studying the packet of material I received from my friend. Focused on the lunch meeting, I felt like David readying for a confrontation with Goliath and like Tom Sawyer preparing to face the likes of Injun Joe. After all, it's not every day that a so-called "abortion person" finds herself on course to dine with someone affiliated with the nation's largest abortion provider. I vividly recall, however, that during those three weeks, I played whack-a-mole with a slew of distractions—petty arguments with Prince Charming, a flareup of asthma in one of the children. *Was someone or something frustrating my efforts? Was I being pushed off task intentionally? Who was trying to intrude on my path of discovery?*

We all have a *Truman Show* moment where all hell ramps up to dissuade us from finding freedom and leaving bondage. The temptation to flee my assignment surfaced, but I was determined to persevere. There was no turning away. Fight prevailed over flight. It's not that I told myself, "You're going to fight this," but the tough-it-out spirit developed in my childhood was on autopilot. The response was automatic. The difference at this point was that it was working in my favor.

As I scrutinized the mountain of information, determined to increase knowledge and courage, a related burden bubbled up and began to weigh on my heart. It was one I couldn't ignore or kick down the road. I sensed the time was ripe for a conversation with the respected pastor of our former church—the one who married Prince Charming and me a decade earlier and the one Gail claimed was supportive of abortion. Initially, I had given him the benefit of the doubt, but I needed to hear his side of the story for confirmation. Calm and collected, I called him at the church and explained the purpose for reaching out.

Suffice it to say he was grateful for my call. With transparency and humility, he shared that many years earlier it was part of the abortion provider's strategy, under the guise of compassion, to build an alliance with and solidify the support of Jewish and Protestant religious leaders for abortion referrals. He recalled he was supportive of adoption, the service they emphasized and claimed to support. This alone attracted him. He confessed he hadn't done his due diligence—the organization *rarely* facilitates adoptions. It didn't take long to break ties with the organization once he realized they hoodwinked him into lending his name. "God," he said, "gives and breathes life." Affiliating with the group, he lamented, was one of the biggest regrets of his career. I believed him.

I'll share another secret with you. Outside of pre-marriage counseling with the respected pastor, the only time I can recall speaking one-on-one with a priest was during childhood. When I was seven years old, I went to my very first scheduled appointment at the church for the express purpose of divulging or admitting an offense—penance. I well remember the anxiety of sitting on a chair, tiny feet dangling, in a tiny, darkened, booth-like room. I sat on one side of a lattice panel and awkwardly confessed to him a fight I had with one of my brothers. The whole ordeal was so nerve-racking and fear-inducing that to claim I shared anything else would be a fabrication made out of thin air. But this I know—the experience that day was a success because, as the expression goes, I killed two birds with one stone. Fighting served two purposes: It was the only thing in my mind weighty enough to qualify for contrition, and it was my ticket out of that confessional. I vowed never again to return—no matter how awful, remorseful, or guilty my conscience felt.

Fast forward. Here I was, a fully grown adult with kids of my own and still fighting. Not fighting in the sense of the hitting and name-calling of yesteryear but fighting to keep my abortion experience buried. Fighting against myself because I had no true or meaningful understanding of the benefits of confession or the freedom that would come by finally dragging the skeleton out of the closet into the light.

Please forgive me if the concepts and terms I've introduced—good and evil, penance, clergy, contrition, God—are not part of your everyday vocabulary. You are not an outsider if the words sound only vaguely familiar or so completely foreign they make you scratch your head. If they cause everything inside you to flash like a neon sign and shout, *"My religion is personal!"* this reaction is alright. It's okay, too, if they pique your interest yet make you feel uncomfortably vulnerable —it's possible you've processed these words in your head but not your heart.

Rest assured, a range of responses is normal. However, as a matter of great importance, might you allow me to get personal for a moment? May I open that forbidden door? May I encourage you, regardless of how this vocabulary affects you, to let go and allow your thinking to expand beyond anything you've ever imagined about God?

Regardless of the health of your relationship with your father here on earth, it's important for you to know God is most definitely *not* a magnified version of him. Would you consider being open to God as a heavenly Father who is *always* loving, *always* good, *always* kind, *always* forgiving, and (cue the megaphone) *always for you*, even if you've experienced abortion? Can you be honest with yourself when I ask, "Where is God in your picture?"

If the question is too difficult or if your pain is still too great, it might be helpful for you to contemplate the truth that a big, sloppy, self-made mess doesn't finish you. In fact, it can be source material for a new beginning. Beauty *can* come from ashes. Consider, for example, how plants recover and emerge after a volcanic eruption. What if allowing God into your box will spring you open in wide-eyed wonder?

I mention God because what we think about Him is important. Ann Lamont magically weaves into metaphor words like tonsils, muscles, cramps, and God to point us in the right direction. She details having her tonsils removed and likens the cramping of the throat muscles around the surgical wound to our psychic muscles that "cramp around our wounds—the pain from our childhood, the losses and disappointments of adulthood, the humiliations suffered in both—to keep us from getting hurt in the same place again." She goes on to say the wounds and cramping we're not even aware of limit us and keep us standing back or backing away from life.

"How do we break through them and get on?" she asks. "It's easier if you believe in God but not impossible if you don't … but he might give you the courage or the stamina." She continues, "Now it might be that your God is an uptight, judgmental perfectionist … I want to caution you away from the standard God of your childhood, who loves and guides you and then, if you are bad, roasts you: God as a high school principal in a gray suit who never remembered your name but is always leafing unhappily through your files. If this is your God, maybe you need to blend in the influence of someone who is ever so slightly more amused by you. … Mr. Rogers will work."[6]

Brennan Manning's perspective on the matter is equally helpful. He posits that many of us "put God on Pier 40 as a niggling customs officer who rifles through our moral suitcase to sort out our deeds, and then hands us a scorecard to tally up virtues and vices, so we can match baseball cards with him on Judgment Day."[7] Elsewhere he asks, "Do you fear this loving and gracious Father? Have you learned to think of the Father as the judge, the spy, the disciplinarian, the punisher? *If you think that way, you're wrong.*"[8]

The Thursday evening before the much anticipated meeting with Gail seemed like any other work and school night. Prince Charming and I read the children their bedtime stories, tucked them in for the night, and called it a day ourselves. He fell asleep right away, but not me! I was a wide-awake, jittery mess, staring at the ceiling and picturing myself walking into the lion's den the next day. A faint sound startled me. Sweet daughter had tiptoed into the bedroom. When our eyes met, she climbed onto the bed, blankie and doll in hand, and complained she didn't feel well. She seized her chance to stay, snuggled, and fell fast asleep. All was well—except for the wiggles part. She was a wiggler and a wriggler and an occasional kickboxer. I started to feel nervous. The threat of a poor night's sleep caused my heart to race even faster, so I gently rolled out of bed and sallied forth to settle into a good night's sleep in her bedroom.

I will forever remember the room—a favorite. For sweet daughter, it was an exciting, newly decorated, big-girl bedroom. For the rest of us, it was an oasis of all-things-little-girl with its soft, colorful floral prints on the bedding and window treatments. Cushions and throw pillows on the white wicker rocking chair wore complementary pink stripes and peeked from underneath her favorite storybooks and a tiered ballet dress trimmed in silk tulle. It had taken me weeks to make the ceramic teapot lamp perched on the nightstand. The gold-framed mirror embellished with groupings of dainty flowers was fastened on the wall above the chest of drawers. It was a unique find intended to see her through her childhood, high school years, and beyond.

The bedroom was a beautiful, happy place that beckoned family and friends to enter the realm of sugar and spice and all that's nice. Surrounded by a supporting audience of sweet daughter's dolls and fluffy stuffed animals waiting at the table for their morning tea party, I felt like a little girl again.

Falling asleep wasn't easy. I tossed and turned and rehearsed likely topics and whatever else this ever-loving earth could serve up at lunch the next day. *How would the conversation start? Who would speak first? Would I choose kindness, knowing our abortion views rested on opposite ends of the spectrum? What motivated her to accept my invitation to lunch? My goodness, would she throw a poison dart?* Saddled with long thoughts about my past and the well-guarded secret, my confidence started to wane. Like a vintage pinball machine, my mind lit up as I sifted through memories of things I had done and things I had left undone. Meanwhile, the hands of the clock on the bedside table waltzed toward early morning. I scrambled to sort out how I had arrived at this point in life. Thoughts shifted. *Who am I? How did all of this come together? The luncheon. THE LUNCHEON? IT'S TWELVE HOURS AWAY! Oh, God!*

Panic rained down in a torrent. My heart skipped a few beats. My nerves were shattered. The clock whirled, and the old, tormenting voice slithered in. *What have you gotten yourself into now? You can't face her. You're a fake and a phony. Virtuous? Ha. No way. Who are you to think you can convince anyone that abortion and religion don't align?*

For the record, I didn't claim to be religious. Or spiritual. I was neither in the sense of reading the Bible or conversing about famous people like David and Moses. Or Jesus, for that matter. Speaking of Jesus, answers to basic questions about Him eluded me. At the risk of sounding irreverent, I didn't understand why He was parked on the cross, with arms stretched wide and the ignition turned off, in the church of my childhood but conspicuously absent on the crosses in the churches of my early adult years. If I had the appearance of piety, it was only because I was a churchgoer. Thanks to my parents who brought me to church, I knew church lingo and what it meant to sit in a pew, kneel, and receive communion. I could recite the Lord's Prayer and "now I lay me down to sleep" kinds of prayers. I could sing from a hymnal and eat doughnuts. Now I was a parent who was convinced that my children needed the godly influence I couldn't give, so I simply did what was modeled for me. Together with Prince Charming, we took them to church.

Church on Sundays for Prince Charming and me had been more of a check-the-box pursuit; however, in recent months, a newfound tenderness had sprung up. Tears, especially during the singing part, would send me rifling through my purse for a Kleenex. Sometimes I'd be so choked up with emotion that I couldn't sing. The sentimentality got my attention. *What is the cause of this? Is my heart breaking? Or is it growing three sizes like the Grinch's?* Frederick Buechner says we don't always know what causes tears, but of this we can be sure: "Whenever you find tears in your eyes, especially unexpected tears, it is well to pay the closest attention. They are not only telling you something about the secret of who you are, but more often than not God is speaking to you through them of the mystery of where you have come from and is summoning you to where, if your soul is to be saved, you should go to next."[9]

I knew *about* God, and I would have pinky-finger promised that in recent days it was God who spoke to me. Nevertheless, I wouldn't have claimed to *know* God like you can know your spouse, child, parent, or friend. As I understood it, that privilege belonged to saintly people. To "good" people. Besides, after all those years of sitting in pews and hearing sermons—pre and post-abortion—*never* did it *ever* cross nor enter my mind that God might absolve a girl's guilt even if she has taken the life of her preborn child. The way I saw it was that taking a life was the most serious of the Ten Commandments, and I didn't even know all the other nine. It seemed to me breaking that one was an absolute, universal no-no, not a universal opinion, even if done in secret. Every soul, every conscience, every culture—whether in a big, flashy city like Tokyo, Japan, or a band society like the Mbuti of the Ituri Rainforest in Central Africa—knows that.

The juxtaposition of *abortion* and *forgiveness* in the same sentence was not something I could have imagined or dreamed about. It was incomprehensible. Abortion—the face-contorting "A" word—was not and still isn't a word used in most churches. I hadn't heard it whispered, even faintly, or spoken or trumpeted by any pulpiteer, old or young. Neither had I heard about the incredible promise that our days of sorrow will end.[10] I most certainly hadn't heard that we don't have to live in darkness and fear because God loves, forgives, and releases women who have experienced abortion.[11] Addictions and mistakes of all kinds—anger, infidelity, divorce, pornography, hatred, gossip, stealing, and lying—were mentioned in many sermons through the years. But teen pregnancy? Crisis pregnancy? Abortion? Nothing. Zero! Zip! Zilch! Nada!

I had no memory of being within earshot of a priest or a pastor extending compassion to us so-called "abortion persons." None had hinted at the truth that failure is a bruise, not a tattoo.[12] Not one insisted that failure is an event, not a person.[13] No one dared to hint there's no pit so deep that God is not deeper still.[14] Hence, all my fleeing, all the running away, the darting, the dabbling, the dodging, the hiding, the secret stuffing and keeping, the constant escaping, and the fear I had lost God forever. For years, I did what Norma McCorvey (Jane Roe) did. I "walked around, casting furtive glances at the sky, wondering when God was going to get fed up and send down a lightning bolt with my name on it."[15]

That night, with all the "star light, star bright, first star I see tonight" little-girl wishing I could do, a heartfelt cry rose from the deepest part of my being. I inhaled and wished for the impossible. I mumbled my greatest desire—for a second chance, a clean slate, another try, a presto-chango moment for everything to be forgiven and forgotten. As I exhaled, I distinctly remember feeling it was safe to let go of the memories and restless thoughts. It was time to stop rehearsing and examining the brokenness. Frederick Buechner eloquently expresses the scene

> "Nobody knows the trouble I've seen" goes the old spiritual, and, of course, nobody knows the trouble we have any of us seen—the hurt,

the sadness, the bad mistakes, the crippling losses—but we know it …
we are to remember it. And then … we will find, beyond any feelings
of joy or regret that one by one the memories give rise to a profound
and undergirding peace, a sense that in some unfathomable way all is
well …

We have survived, you and I. Maybe that is at the heart of our
remembering. After twenty years, forty years, sixty years, or eighty,
we have made it to this year, this day. We needn't have made it. There
were times we never thought we would and nearly didn't. There were
times we almost hoped we wouldn't, were ready to give the whole
thing up.

To remember my life is to remember countless times when I might
have given up, gone under, when humanly speaking I might have
gotten lost beyond the power of any to find me. But I didn't. I have not
given up. And each of you, with all the memories you have and the
tales you could tell, you also have not given up. You also are survivors
and are here. And what does that tell us, our surviving? It tells us that
weak as we are, a strength beyond our strength has pulled us through
at least this far, at least to this day.

Foolish as we are, a wisdom beyond our wisdom has flickered up
just often enough to light us if not to the right path through the forest,
at least to a path that leads forward, that is bearable. Faint of heart as
we are, a love beyond our power to love has kept our hearts alive."[16]

If there was even the slightest hope of falling asleep, surrender was
imperative. Looking heavenward, believing like a child that maybe
God was within earshot, I accepted ownership of my powerlessness
and neediness. I got straight to the point and said aloud, "God, I need
sleep for tomorrow. I prepared the best way I knew how, but I'm
afraid. I don't know what I'm doing, and I can't do this on my own. I
need You. I *really really* do need You."

I didn't feel the need to make myself more presentable. Nothing I
said was eloquent or rehearsed. It was just broken me in my pajamas,
uttering something short, simple, and raw. I prayed with the kind of
trust "little Diane" had once enjoyed when talking to her daddy in the

years before the war, before the sweet connection was fractured. Brennan Manning says, "Getting honest with ourselves does not make us unacceptable to God. It does not distance us from God but draws us to Him—as nothing else can—and opens us anew to the flow of grace. While Jesus calls each of us to a more perfect life, we cannot achieve it on our own. To be alive is to be broken; to be broken is to stand in need of grace."[17]

I raised the white flag and surrendered. Tears rolled down my cheeks.

I closed my eyes but kept my internal gaze toward Heaven. I was exhausted. As I released my burdens and cares and let go of the weight and responsibility of my life, the impossibilities, the pressures, the tormenting thoughts, unbelief, fears, and worry, it felt as though someone was enfolding me and drawing me near. The next moment, in the velvet of night, I was swept into and overcome by mystery—the palpable presence of love. A love more real and more penetrating than I had ever experienced. A love that seemed to say, "I know you. I know everything about you. And I accept you." I felt safe but didn't move. My eyes opened up in wonder. I then heard a gentle whisper speak slowly and directly to my heart, "I forgive you."

Everything inside me quickened. I recognized the voice immediately. It was the same tender voice that addressed me by name when I was a girl. The one that assured me Dad loved me the way he *knew* how to love me. I knew that I knew that I knew it was the voice of God. Not only that, I felt His presence—the presence of the God of the universe. The God I had run from for too many years had just spoken to me again. And I knew, without a doubt, He was referring to the abortion, the very *last* offense I thought would qualify for forgiveness.

I was experiencing His mercy and relentless tenderness. In one heart-twisting, mind-bending moment, I had received the gift of God's grace—His pardon from sin and all the mess. The threat of punishment vanished like yesteryear's nightmare. The acquittal was nothing I earned. It was nothing I deserved. Borrowing Brennen Manning's words, "I experienced the forgiveness of Jesus not as the reprieve of a judge but the embrace of a lover. I was liberated from pettiness, self-centeredness, and fear. I was purified in the darkness of faith, beyond belief."[18]

Indeed, my fear of God's anger was stripped away. I didn't have the urge to run away but to stay put, externally and internally. In the twinkling of an eye, I had been awakened to the fact that God knew every detail of my life. Every secret. He met me where I was—lost and surrendered. As my mind raced with such thoughts, a brilliant light appeared before me. It wasn't blinding, but there was no mistaking I was being drawn into the radiant nearness of a Holy God. As I looked to the light, humbled and speechless, I received an understanding in the deepest reaches of my soul that what I had done as a seventeen-year-old was ultimately not against the baby or me or anyone else but against God Himself. My heart was pierced. Tears flowed like a fountain.

With stark, raving honesty—one-on-one—I acknowledged the pain and gently cried with godly sorrow, "Oh God! I did that against You. I sinned against *You*. Oh God, I am so, so, very, very sorry."

No combination of words can adequately describe what happened next. The experience started with what felt like a miraculous cleansing of the abortion. After that, the debris and chaos that had attached itself to me through all of my ignorant, unholy, and foolish choices and behaviors vanished. The dross was pulled away. The slithering, tormenting voice was silenced. Like a judge who rules, "Charges dismissed and expunged," God removed it all. There was freedom. Peace and hope flooded my heart, and I was surprised by unspeakable joy. Everything inside me felt renewed, like a rebirth. I came to life!

The next morning, as I walked into the hallway from sweet daughter's bedroom, I came face-to-face with Prince Charming. Searching for an intelligent way to express the inexpressible, I looked into his eyes and said, "Something crazy happened to me last night. I don't have the words or the ability to explain it, but what I do know is that I'm not the same person I was before going to bed last night. And I don't want to argue with you anymore."

Liz Wright perfectly encapsulates the entire encounter, "The most important moment in life is when we experience the love of God. This is what changes everything."[19]

A REFLECTION

"We are children, perhaps, at the very moment when we know that it is as children that God loves us—not because we have deserved his love and not in spite of our undeserving; not because we try and not because we recognize the futility of our trying; but simply because he has chosen to love us. We are children because he is our father; and all our efforts, fruitful and fruitless, to do good, to speak truth, to understand, are the efforts of children who, for all their precocity, are children still in that before we loved him, he loved us, as children, through Jesus Christ our Lord."[20]

Eugene Peterson beckons us to believe that hearing is a skill that can renew our lives. He says,

Your listening ear is the most responsible gift you can bring. Listening is not only a function of biological acoustics; it is a spiritual skill of the soul. There is something being said to you ... something said that is designed to rule your life, to lead you into a new way of existence, something that can evoke a response that has eternal dimensions to it ... that says you are loved by God, that you are accepted by God, that your life has an eternal meaning and destiny. ... Once you hear that, you will never hear anything old again. Everything will be new.[21]

My experience with the relentless tenderness of God came not while advocating for the sanctity of life. Not while sitting in a pew in a church. Not while attending a religious ceremony. Not while singing hymns or reading a spiritual book. It came while lying quietly on sweet daughter's bed, waiting and listening for a response from the God I didn't yet know.

Friend, if He did this for me, please believe He can, He will, and He desires to do the same for you. May I encourage you to separate yourself from the noise and believe God will speak to you too. Forgiveness and love and hope await you.

P.S. You are loved.

NINE

White as Snow

"It's IMPOSSIBLE"...said reason
"It's RISKY"...said experience.
"It's POINTLESS"...said pride.
"GIVE IT A TRY"...whispered the heart.
—Unknown—

MEET HIROO ONODA. THE ONCE OBSCURE WWII JAPANESE SOLDIER needlessly squandered time and purpose fighting a decades-long private war. His story, in part, reliably parallels women on the battleground of abortion and the complexity of our journey to freedom.

His autobiography *No Surrender: My Thirty-Year War* chronicles his thoughts, his will to survive, and his ability to outmaneuver all his pursuers. It's a telling narrative demonstrating the power of deception and the sorrowful consequences of refusing to believe our private war is over. It also illustrates at least three choices we face as we survey our lives on the battlefield. We can grovel in pride, bitterness, and denial, ignoring the hand that reaches out to help. We can continue in our unfreedom, blame everyone but ourselves, take hits from those on each side of the battle, and die in the line of duty clenching our guilty conscience, shame, and self-loathing. Or we can turn from the gritty routine of half-living and walk into forgiveness, healing, and a new realm of possibility—living our best life!

In December 1944, the young intelligence officer, Onada, was sent to Lubang Island, Philippines, to lead guerilla operations and hamper the enemy's attack on the island. Within two short months, after U.S. and Philippine forces had taken the island, only he and three other Japanese soldiers were alive. They took to the jungle. Six months later (August 1945), the small band of hidden holdouts was surprised to find a leaflet announcing Japan's surrender and the war's end. They concluded the notice was bogus and refused to believe the news. Months afterward, a plane dropped leaflets with printed orders to surrender. In 1949, one of the soldiers, Yuichi Akatsu, deserted the other three. Years later, another plane dropped family photos and letters urging surrender—all to no avail. The stragglers distrusted the authenticity of the evidence and concluded the communications were propaganda and trickery. They refused to surrender and continued with their guerilla activities. Over time, two of the remaining three were shot and killed leaving Onoda as the sole survivor—that is, until a young adventurer named Norio Suzuki found and persuaded him to consider that the war had ended. He surrendered weeks later, in March 1974, after nearly thirty years in the jungle.

As David Kupelian says, sometimes self-deception, like a rubber band, can be stretched only so far before it either breaks or snaps back to normal.[1]

In the final chapters of *No Surrender*, Onoda recounts meeting Suzuki. Suzuki's kindness and sincerity inclined Onoda to consider a truer message—the life-saving promise that the war was over. He became receptive and listened to someone who *wasn't* delusional once he was freed from the influence of his "fight the war at any cost" friends. (Do you have such friends?) Onoda explains how difficult it was to ignore the young man's explanation of how things *really* were. While ninety-nine percent was unbelievable, the remaining one percent drove the holdout into a quandary.

Finally, Onoda told Suzuki that because he risked his life to come to the island, he would gamble on Suzuki's truthfulness. He rolled the dice on the one percent—a bold choice that sparked his rescue! Soon after, Onoda's former commanding officer returned to Lubang, officially ordered him to cease military activities, and relieved him of duty. After his official surrender, he was escorted from the island back to his homeland. As the helicopter lifted into flight, questions plagued Onoda as he looked down on his battlefield for the first time. *Why had I fought here for thirty years? Who had I been fighting for? What was the cause?*[2]

Be encouraged, friend. Questions like Onoda asked after his rescue echo in our minds. It's certainly true of my story. We pay an enormous cost when we rely on our own understanding and mistrust truth-tellers who point us to the way out and the way off the battlefield. May I plead with you to trust that my account of how things *really* are is honest and trustworthy? Consider pursuing the prospect of restored hope in your heart, the route to joy and the benefits of mercy—even if, like Onoda, you're hesitant or afraid. Take a gamble and experience *the* remedy, *the* solution, *the* elixir. Encounter *the* One who offers the rich and meaningful life you long for and leave the battlefield behind you, never to return.

In the days, weeks, and months following my genuine reset in sweet daughter's bedroom, life moved on an excitingly new trajectory. I was a work in progress, but the transformation was profound. God's extravagant love and a settled, confident hope have this effect.

"Not guilty" proved to be the catalyst for the expansion of heartfelt happiness and goodness—for myself, Prince Charming, and our children. I began to see and hear things in a brand new way. Life's rhythm exploded from lackluster black and white into textured, living color. Putting words to it was the greatest challenge, so I exercised my sense of exploration to understand the turnaround. Mostly, I read books that friends recommended and listened to messages on Christian radio while driving the children to and from school.

If you're murmuring, "That sounds too good to be true!" you're right. Well, partially right. Grace is a gift far beyond what our simple, collective human intellect can comprehend. Madeleine L'Engle once said, "We are suspicious of grace. We are afraid of the very lavishness of the gift."[3] What is grace? Frederick Buechner says it like this:

> Grace is never something you can get but can only be given. There's no way to earn it or deserve it or bring it about any more than you can deserve the taste of raspberries and cream or earn good looks or bring about your own birth.
>
> A crucial eccentricity of the Christian faith is the assertion that people are saved by grace. There's nothing *you* have to do. There's nothing you *have* to do. There's nothing you have to *do*.
>
> The grace of God means something like: Here is your life. You might never have been, but you are because the party wouldn't have been complete without you. Here is the world. Beautiful and terrible things will happen. Don't be afraid. I am with you. Nothing can ever separate us. It's for you I created the universe. I love you.
>
> There's only one catch. Like any other gift, the gift of grace can be yours only if you'll reach out and take it.[4]

I want to be equally transparent and tell you that even though my experience was revolutionary, it was most definitely *not* a shortcut to emotional health. The sting of my abortion history was gone. Guilt had been removed as if it had never happened. However, the memory of it continued to follow me like Pig-Pen's little dust cloud. It nipped at my heels and encircled me in unworthiness. The longing to run with an outward confidence reflecting the new me was tethered, taut, and hindered. Nicole Zasowski writes, "Painful messages that we are alone, inadequate, and worthless will loiter longer in our brains than the truth: that we are valuable, prized, and full of worth."[5] Being pardoned was one matter. I had come to know and believe God's love for me. The issue yet to be grappled with was the mystery of my soul—my mind, will, and emotions—and the need for intentional healing of this part of my humanness.

As noted earlier, we remain on the battlefield for many reasons.

While some women deny outright any and all harm, a growing number of professional and lay counselors are helping to spotlight the truth that abortion is, in fact, a trauma that inflicts unseen, internal wounds. These must be addressed head-on to open the door to the healing and wholeness intended for us and to repair the foundation of our true identity. The wounds cannot be ignored, glossed over, or smothered. They don't erode over time. Putting cheap paint over rust might work for a season, but the rust will win in the end.[6]

My struggle with what is known today as Post Abortion Stress Syndrome (PASS)—the residual pain and subconscious effects of abortion—was real. I was shackled to the invisible chains of stigma and shame. I was hemmed in by unresolved grief. At the time, if anyone was whispering or talking about these feelings and repercussions, all communication must have been behind closed doors. Compassionate discourse wasn't readily available. Neither was there a frenzied push for open conversation about the "diversity of abortion experiences" or a public crusade to erase negative consequences.

But that was then and this is now. Today, there are a number of books, workbooks, workshops, and retreats addressing freedom and offering beneficial healing. Meaningful, tenderhearted conversation and transformational counseling are available. Regrettably, truthful information faces a three-pronged challenge. First, emotional paralysis, ignorance, and fear keep many women from searching for it. Second, an online exploration of psychological outcomes of abortion isn't simple—it requires a determined deep dive to find helpful results. Finally, there seems to be a concerted effort by "experts" in government, medical and mental health clinicians, and their ivory tower research friends to disregard PASS. They even go so far as to claim PASS is non-existent, a myth, or a rumor.

There's nothing new under the sun. Here's an interesting side note: This same bastion of intellect—though different people and a different war—turned their backs on hundreds of thousands of men experiencing psychological and psychosomatic symptoms after returning home from WWI. The powers that be initially created a diagnosis called "shell shock," a type of post-traumatic stress disorder (PTSD), but then revoked it. They changed their mind and asserted the root cause of the men's severe disturbances was not active warfare but a pre-war experience. None of us should be surprised that a similar proposition is made about us women who struggle after abortion. The pundits' refusal to consider our signs and symptoms and their insistence that our pre-war troubles are the source of our angst do not negate our personal suffering.

On the flip side of the coin, there's plenty of chatter rationalizing and justifying abortion. In an effort to divert and deflect valid anxiety and apprehension, for example, pre-abortion counseling in some clinics has shifted to include mention of social stigma and shame. No time is wasted, however, for the procedure to then be propped up and pushed as the healthy, perfectly normal choice. One clinic loudly and proudly claims that every day, *good* women have abortions.[7] This approach might help reduce objections, but ultimately it inspires more abortions and traps women in deceit, diversion, and cul-de-sacs. It does nothing to prevent or hamper distress or any other unforeseen negative risk and cost.

As someone who descended to the deep waters of life and endured darkness and despair, I attest to the accuracy and truthfulness of Stephen Covey's claim: "We are free to choose our actions, but we are not free to choose the consequences of these actions."[8]

Many women try to dismantle stigma and shame by blame-shifting. Unwavering in their claim that abortion is inherently linked to feminism and the women's liberation movement, they accuse the culture, law and government, paternalism, and everyone else for the troublesome emotions associated with the procedure. They reject the idea of personal responsibility. Others attempt to intellectualize and minimize these emotions with enlightened-sounding articles published online and in women's magazines. Self-help books and secular, nonsensical counseling attempt to deconstruct or eradicate stigma and shame but leave women in a holding pattern of helplessness and distress. One movement afoot encourages women to publicly combat abortion's negative social stigma by "shouting their abortion" on social media. More than anything, though, this kind of campaign amounts to window dressing: It might bolster women in the moment to feel brave and victorious while sharing their stories, but it invariably leaves them feeling empty and naked and running for cover.

And yet, here's the core of the matter: Every self-willed effort to confront, scrub, or cleanse abortion's muck and mire from an external perspective is powerless to eradicate and permanently allay the internal strife, remorse, and woe that cry for relief. It's possible to find sincerity and empathy behind the loudest voices perpetuating denial or claiming antidotes—but buyer beware! If messages lack any mention of substantive, guilt-free, lasting healing, their promises are just Band-Aids that are sure to fall off in tomorrow's shower. Like false gods who blow wind and confusion, they do nothing to address our wounds or the struggle in our hearts.

Attention! This is the leaflet I'm dropping into the warzone: THE WAR *IS* OVER! THERE *IS* A WAY TO REPAIR WHAT HAPPENED. THERE *IS* GREAT PROMISE FOR OUR FUTURE. THERE *IS* A REMEDY THAT BRINGS TRANSFORMATION.

It is never too late to leave the past behind and walk into a richer and more shimmering life. In the words of George Eliot, "It's never too late to shine."[9]

Before I tell you about the second significant event of my transformation, it's important to candidly address and dissect post-abortion feelings and emotions. Why? You may ask. Because the battlefield is littered with heavy-laden souls and troubled hearts sitting in shadows of the unknown. It's time to bring light to darkness and illuminate the truth. Aside from physical risks, whether or not we or the so-called experts are willing to admit it, abortion is a trauma often followed by emotional pain and a sense of foreboding. Without fail, it's invariably accompanied by a haunting guilt, stigma, and shame. Despite anybody's best efforts to deny or downplay the harmful effects of abortion, it's never a stand-alone event.

A *trauma* is an unutterable experience that is outside the human ability to handle or understand on our own. A normal response is to try to forget it, run from it, repress it, or conceal it—whatever it takes to avoid the horrible experience and quell the memory of it. Dr. Burke points out that though we attempt to avoid dealing with distress, an equally powerful human need to understand and find meaning in our experiences is at work. She contends:

> While a person may consciously choose to avoid thinking about the traumatic experience, his or her subconscious insists on calling attention to the trauma. The subconscious knows that an unresolved trauma is unfinished business. In order to be conquered, the horror of the traumatic event must be exposed, proclaimed, and understood. This tension between the need to hide a trauma and the need to expose it is at the heart of many of the psychological symptoms resulting from abortion.
>
> More simply put, women who suffer from post-abortion problems want to avoid and deny those problems while at the same time seeking resolution and peace of heart. These two needs are working at cross purposes.[10]

Dr. Bessel van der Kolk is a medical doctor and leading specialist on trauma. He has spent over three decades studying and working with survivors. His scientific research, detailed in his bestselling book *The Body Keeps the Score,* describes how a traumatic experience transforms us: It leaves an imprint and affects how we live in the present. Not only that, he explains how it literally reshapes the brain, mind, and body. His work is important because he validates the symptoms of trauma and offers hope for reclaiming our lives.[11]

Guilt is the responsibility for wrongdoing. It convicts us in the court of our own conscience and leaves us with a sense of condemnation, looming punishment, or judgment. Unless we have dulled or hardened our hearts, the feeling distinguishes and shouts the rightness or wrongness of our choices and behaviors. Like physical pain, it's a signal feeling prodding us to stop and to express and resolve problems we have experienced. Even if we genuinely approached abortion as a simple removal of "tissue" or the "products of conception," we will eventually be unable to ignore our remorse and culpability. Guilt is real, not just a mental state of mind or hysteria.

No mere human can conceal, erase, or, like the Landing Signal Officer, wave off guilt. We cannot wish it away or talk our way out of it. There's no soap strong enough to remove it. It's not temporary—it lingers. It's a stain that goes deep into the spiritual fabric of the soul and inevitably oppresses, cripples, and enslaves us. It pierces the heart and negatively impacts our self-image and self-worth. Frederick Buechner says it this way, "It is about as hard to absolve yourself of your own guilt as it is to sit in your own lap."[12]

Denial and rationalization are not effective means of dealing with real guilt. The only effective cure for real guilt is real forgiveness. Emancipation comes only when we honestly examine what we have done and confess it. I can tell you with certainty that God forgives anyone who's sincerely sorry. Though what I had done could not be undone, I was forgiven. You can have this same confidence. If you confess, God will forgive you and cleanse your guilty conscience.[13]

Stigma, in the figurative sense, is a word commonly used today to refer to a negative stereotype or reputation attached to something.[14] It hits us from the outside and confers a mark of public disgrace and dishonor. It's like Hester Prynne's token of infamy in *The Scarlet Letter*. Visible to all, the "A" (signifying adultery) on the bodice of her gown cast a lurid gleam of awe and horrible repugnance round about her and caused people to shudder.[15] Surprisingly, seven years of wearing it didn't lessen its effect. It's worth noting that when it comes to abortion, nothing has diluted the strong sense of external disapproval —neither the high number of annual abortions, the fact that millions upon millions have experienced them (directly or indirectly), nor the extent to which people go to reframe the way culture talks about the procedure. To borrow the words of counselor and author Dr. Edward Welch, "It doesn't matter that so many others have experienced these things…misery doesn't care if it has company. Lepers might live in the same colony, but they share no vibrant community."[16]

More agonizing than the stigma exerted by others is the imprint of abortion's hidden, internal mark on our spirits. From the Greek word of the same spelling, *stigma* means "mark of a pointed instrument, puncture, tattoo-mark, brand."[17] Noah Webster defines this kind of stigma as "a brand; a mark made with a burning iron; any mark of infamy; or any reproachful conduct which stains the purity or darkens the luster of reputation."[18]

Since 1840, Nathaniel Hawthorne has provided a vivid example in the Reverend Mr. Dimmesdale. When he finally announces himself as the father of Hester's daughter Pearl, he tells the townspeople Hester's scarlet letter, "with all its mysterious horror, is but the shadow of what he bears on his own breast and that his own red stigma is no more than what has seared his inmost heart."[19] His admission rightly reveals both the reality and agony of spiritual stigma and the need to bring it to the surface and into the disinfecting light. Why? Because no amount of secrecy, no voice of reason, no eating disorder, no self-convincing affirmation of this-was-right-for-me or abortion-is-love or abortion-is-mercy, no headstrong pull-yourself-together, no busyness, and no psychiatric drugs or mood-altering alcohol can dispel its ache and anguish.

Shame is defined as a "painful sensation excited by a consciousness of guilt or by the exposure of that which nature or modesty prompts us to conceal"[20] It is so insidious that it deserves—if not necessitates—a thorough explanation. As Dr. Dan Allender explains, "Shame has been called by Jean-Paul Sartre 'a hemorrhage of the soul.' It is an awful experience to be aware that we are (or might be) seen as deficient and undesirable by someone whom we hope will deeply enjoy us."[21] Indeed, following abortion, it joins arms with stigma and becomes another agonizing, paralyzing symptom that drives us into hiding.

In *Shame Interrupted,* Dr. Welch describes the feeling as "the deep sense that you are unacceptable because of something you did, something that was done to you, or something associated with you. You feel exposed and humiliated. Or, to strengthen the language, you are disgraced because you acted less than human, you were treated as less than human, or you were associated with something less than human and there are witnesses."[22]

He further describes shame as "life-dominating and stubborn. Once entrenched in your heart and mind, it is a squatter that refuses to leave … you *never* laugh at it … it becomes your identity … it touches everything about you."[23] A quiet killer and an elusive heart disease, shame is problematic because there is no gradual way to deal with it.[24] In other words, it cannot be removed or erased by any number or combination of therapeutic coping mechanisms. Shame affects us spiritually and, therefore, calls for a deeply spiritual solution to break its power over us and open us to great hope.[25]

In a world that's confused about spirituality and God, you might be thinking He will only further complicate things. You're not alone— many post-abortive women have a distorted image of God. I did. I want to assure you, though, this is *wrong thinking*. The truth is "He is compassionate and merciful, slow to get angry, and filled with unfailing love. He will not constantly accuse us, nor remain angry forever. He does not punish us for all our sins; he does not deal harshly with us, as we deserve" (Psalm 103:8–10 NLT). He is not ashamed of us. His understanding is something we cannot fathom. We *need* the acceptance and assurance of the One who created us. He sees our scar tissue. He already knows every detail of our lives. He knows our names. He has gazed into the depths of our hearts, and still, He loves us. Better yet, He's in the business of pinpointing, uprooting, and casting out negative emotions and uncovering every lie we've believed. He redeems our broken hearts.

Albert Schweitzer once said, "At times our own light goes out and is rekindled by a spark from another person. Each of us has cause to think with deep gratitude of those who have lighted the flame within us."[26] I will forever be indebted to Georgette, a friend whose spark rekindled my flame. The story I'm about to tell you is how she was used as a vessel of love and empathy to lead me to victory over the latent shame, stigma, and unresolved grief that had tied me in unsolvable knots for far too long. Ta-da! This is my account of the second major event in my transformation.

After months of walking in forgiveness, I had the intuition, the flair to open my heart and disclose my past with Prince Charming. Pinching doubt tempted me to remain silent, but I knew honest self-disclosure was paramount. Keeping anything concealed wasn't truthful or healthy for either of us or for our marriage. I knew being transparent was the right and honorable thing to do, regardless of how difficult it was. So one quiet morning, in response to a gentle nudge, I sat down beside him and dove headfirst into confessing the secret I had so scrupulously kept. Be encouraged, friend. He didn't fall to pieces. He didn't hit the roof, either. His response? It was leagues beyond what I could have anticipated—twenty-thousand leagues!

The way he fixed his gaze on my tear-filled eyes, listened, and asked questions with tenderheartedness and kindness awakened my long-buried self-worth. His ability to embrace my vulnerability and accept me in light of all the brokenness and ugliness effectively called forth in me dignity and value that had been diminished for decades. That he affirmed me and didn't recoil in horror endeared him to me more deeply than ever. The entire experience was far beyond anything I ever dreamed possible. Trust me when I tell you the heart-to-heart conversation I feared would be *the* biggest threat to our marriage and family became a pivotal turning point and a buttress of trust and strength. It was so liberating that it made me wonder why I hadn't told him sooner.

One day, after several weeks of observing the "new me," Prince Charming wondered aloud if I had considered the value of sharing my story and helping other women step into freedom. My reply? *Gulp! What on earth?* The idea terrified me to the core. After all, I was still enjoying the rest and relief of scaling Mt. Secrecy with him. His vote of confidence might have been reassuring, but, admittedly, fear and inadequacy reigned. I needed more time and heaps more courage and resilience before stepping into the limelight. Judgment from others was a worrisome obstacle.

More importantly, I wouldn't have dared to open up with strangers before opening the door of my secret closet to my VIPs—namely my parents, my children, my family, and best friends—who rightfully deserved to hear my story before anyone else. The timing of these conversations had to feel right and be right. He wholeheartedly agreed but encouraged me to be on the lookout for opportunities that would come my way—one woman at a time. He also reminded me about the gift of leading others to the freedom of confession—a word that seems frightening and difficult unless we tune in to what confession truly is: "To confess your sins to God is not to tell him anything He doesn't already know. Until you confess them, however, they are the abyss between you. When you confess them, they become the Golden Gate Bridge."[27]

Life was humming along when, out of the blue, I remembered an organization I had discovered during my research days. Part of the mission of the Silent No More Awareness Campaign is to acknowledge the devastating effects of abortion and promote healing of the secret emotional, physical, and spiritual pain it causes.[28] The group aims to educate the public about the truth of abortion's long-term, negative consequences. Personal testimonies of those who regret their abortions and wish to break the silence ("silent no more") provide evidence that confronting our abortion secrets is necessary if we want to avoid the penalty of remaining forever a prisoner of the secrecy. Courage spurs courage.

Even though I didn't yet have the confidence to share my story, I got a wild hair idea to invite a member from the group to speak at the church. I took a chance, shared my vision with the pastor's wife, and asked if she would consider supporting my efforts. I'll forever remember the excitement of her reply because, honestly, I don't know which one of us was more surprised. She told me she would support the idea, help organize the visit, and personally call Georgette (one of the co-founders) because they were good friends. I still smile whenever I think about how those details seemed to have been worked together before I even asked. A coincidence? I think not.

Fast forward. Georgette journeyed to our church for a weekend-long visit. The starting point was a Saturday morning gathering with a small group of women and men (yes, men!) with whom she addressed her experience and her work with Silent No More. During Sunday's regular morning service, she taught about God's forgiveness and redemption for those struggling with the trauma and aftermath of abortion. She presented her story and drew parallels with the biblical account of first-century religious people who caught a woman in the very act of adultery and brought her to Jesus in public. Cemented in self-righteousness and raising fingers of accusation, they were prepared to stone her to death—the prescribed and lawful punishment of the day—but paused to ask Jesus how they should respond to her immoral behavior.

Jesus faced the frenzied crowd and brilliantly redirected their focus by telling them that stone throwing was only permissible for those who were without sin. Their response was striking. *Not a single stone was thrown.* Every man dropped his stone and sauntered away leaving only Jesus and the woman at the scene. With the jury gone, He looked at her with unrivaled love, told her He didn't condemn her, then directed her to go and sin no more. In other words, in the blink of an eye, she was acquitted. Not guilty. She received the gift of *no condemnation,* just like that. Bingo![29]

Georgette concluded her teaching with good news that grace—God's aggressive forgiveness—is available to the disgraced. Jesus, she declared, responds in our day with equal compassion and tenderness to women who have experienced abortion. He's not in the judgment business. For our failure and flaws, He is rich in mercy.

A hush fell over the sanctuary. It was palpable. No doubt, those seated in the polished, wooden pews wrestled with a medley of emotions and convictions. Whether abortion had touched their lives in one way or another or not at all, I'm sure some fought back tears. More than a handful probably squirmed as they processed the shock of Georgette's transparency and the use of the "A" word in church.

Perhaps others—the unstained, undamaged, tidy, self-satisfied type—quietly sputtered their protests and indignation and wondered why anyone with a history of abortion would be worthy of heaven. I cried happy tears knowing God was watching and looking for humble-hearted women—to lift them up and rescue them from the misery of battlefield-brokenness. He doesn't lose track of anyone. His eyes are always on us. He delights to end our suffering and bless us. His heart is always reaching out to us. Friend, He likes people like us.

At the end of Georgette's talk, she invited everyone seeking forgiveness or desiring healing to join her for the final scheduled event —a Sunday evening healing service. My plan to participate that night was carefully orchestrated and uncomplicated. Originally I hadn't arranged to attend, but since I had organized the weekend, it was both sensible and polite for me to be there. Already "forgiven and fine," I would simply show up, quietly observe from the back of the chapel, and learn firsthand how to lead women into the forgiving arms of God. If needed, I was prepared to extend empathy and caring hugs of comfort. Then I would return home. Simple. Safe.

The real event was much different. Prince Charming, always supportive, insisted that he accompany me that cloudy winter night. We entered the small, dimly-lit chapel and realized we were part of a very intimate group. It was obvious there would be no spectating from the sidelines, so to speak. Georgette welcomed everyone and described her vision for the evening—how she would lead participants, confidentially, into a time of inner healing and freedom.

It hadn't entered my mind that God might have intentions for me. Like Hirro Onoda, I was still fighting my silent war of PASS. Admittedly, I wasn't as "fine" as I thought I was. I had a deep, unhealed wound I didn't even suspect. I had no idea abortion is like origami—where unfolding one part exposes other parts that are more tightly folded. But God knows. He's a gentleman who addresses our pain in stages and heals in layers as we can handle it. He knows that reversing everything at once is as overwhelming as a good-for-nothing avalanche. Little did I know I was about to encounter His relentless pursuit to bring healing to my mind, memory, will, and emotions and to uproot and lift years of secret grief.

After Georgette finished talking, one gal, so touched and so moved by the morning's teaching, bluntly admitted her readiness to receive forgiveness and healing and anything else God would give her. Like an eager classroom student racing to answer a question, her boldness seemed to set the tone for the evening. Everything inside me was cheering for her. That is, until I was ambushed by a strident voice. *Don't admit your history. You'll be judged and exposed as a hypocrite.* The words jarred me then coursed through my veins: *Don't admit anything. Hold back. You don't want them to know. You're fine. Just listen.*

You need to know, friend, that shame will block your windpipe and strangle you if it detects you're about to come out of hiding or shed your negative self-image or discover your true dignity and identity. I determined, on the spot, it was safer to keep quiet. Then, in a New York second, the other woman, through an eruption of wailing and tears, confessed her need for help—not from just one abortion but two.

Her admission shocked me. I was almost undone. The voice from outside slithered in again and brought condemnation and accusations— not against me but against her. *Two? That's horrendous. How could anyone have more than one? You're sitting pretty compared to that! Keep your secret.* I sat motionless. Bound to silence. Until the words of Max Lucado bubbled up and flared forth. In *He Chose the Nails,* he explains how every member of humanity starts out in an identical condition. We're born with the problem of sin and the struggle with depravity—there's not a single exception. He amplifies the danger for those caught in the snare of comparison and pride:

> They look around and say, "Compared to everyone else I'm a decent person." You know, a pig might say something similar. He might look at his trough partners and announce, "I'm just as clean as everyone else." Compared to humans, however, that pig needs help. Compared to God we humans need the same. The standard for sinlessness isn't

found at the pig troughs of earth but at the throne of heaven. God, himself, is the standard.[30]

There I was. Virtue signaling. Like Max's sanctimonious pig, I was playing the comparison game.

In that moment, the familiar, loving voice firmly informed my heart that I needed more of God's help. I reasoned with myself. *Here I am. This is a safe place and a safe gathering of the most authentic, caring, compassionate people on the planet. Why shouldn't I take the risk? Am I coming to the end of myself?*

The shouting match inside my head roared and intensified like the one the Reverend Mr. Dimmesdale must have heard before publicly disclosing his secret. Like him, I fought back weakness and faintness of heart. A gentle whisper filled my inmost being, *"Try."*

The urge to speak was so strong I couldn't avoid it. In front of everyone, I abandoned constraint and came out of hiding. I looked at them and publicly admitted my need for God's healing touch. The secret was out. I dropped my head into my hands. Tears turned to sobbing. Light had penetrated the darkness.

As you can imagine, a measure of shock and anguish filled the chapel after the imposter stepped forward. But Georgette, with skill and lovingkindness, met and handled the development with understanding and wholehearted care for everyone assembled. There was no shame or judgment. Like a gentle shepherd, she tenderly gathered us closer and brought calm and order to the chaotic, jumbled group situation. She gave us permission to share our feelings freely. "By creating room for those around us to be honest," says Floyd McClung, "we can lead them into a deeper relationship with God. … Giving people the opportunity to be honest gives them the security to be honest not only about their emotions but also their needs."[31] Admitting our need publicly, Georgette told us, was the most difficult but most necessary first step through the doorway into God's presence. Indeed, breakdowns lead to breakthroughs and His incomparably great, transforming strength and power.

For the remainder of our time together, Georgette led us on a journey to healing. She assured us that the work of exploring our secrets—the gut-wrenching work with tear-soaked tissues strewn all over the floor to prove it—would remove the weight of our burdens. Processing the reality of what had happened would give way to an inner peace and wholeness we couldn't have imagined. God did not disappoint! His understanding is inscrutable.

We also memorialized our unborn children as He carried away our hidden grief for the little ones we never held. Then came the most favorable, hope-filled gift—one I hadn't considered before. We were given the revelation of what happened to our preborn children. We learned our children are in heaven and that we will see them one day.

In his best-selling book *Heaven*, Randy Alcorn suggests that many people will meet their children lost to abortion and miscarriage. He believes we will be reunited with them and experience the joy of watching them grow up. "Perhaps," he says, "these children will grab our hands and show us around the present heaven."[32]

As God dismantled shame and shattered all stigma, He gave us newness of life. He restored our inner freedom and deposited hope into our lives. He granted us a sense of true belonging. In the words of Brennan Manning, "He brought to the heart of our wounds the balm of acceptance and love."[33]

Humbled and strengthened, we expressed gratitude and exchanged hugs with the group before leaving. As Prince Charming and I opened the door to exit the chapel, we paused and stood in wonder and awe—a fresh blanket of snow covered everything. Gently falling snowflakes left us speechless. Neither of us had seen a winter storm in the weather forecast. For me, it was an exclamation point and a real-time metaphor for God's proclamation over what He had done. He imprinted on my mind and heart what He spoke long ago through the prophet Isaiah, "Though your sins are like scarlet, I will make them as white as snow. Though they are red like crimson, I will make them as white as wool" (Isaiah 1:18 NLT).

A REFLECTION

Can you feel hope rising? If so, do not fear. God is chasing after and pursuing beautiful you. Turn to Him. The cure for our struggles—full vindication—has everything to do with how we become connected to Him.

There is a time in the wedding service when the bride and groom face each other. It is a moment heavy with meaning. The bride and groom are turning away from all others and have eyes for each other alone. They are face-to-face. In a similar way, your life changes when a king turns his face toward you. It means he is going to act favorably on your behalf. When the King (Jesus) turns his face to you, it means that blessing is on the way. It means he is committed to you and will be faithful as you live under his protection. ... God turns to you as a sign of His favor. You, in response, turn toward Him and begin to reflect His beauty. Other people begin to realize that you are with the King. You are starting to look beautiful, like the glorious King. [34]

"I prayed to the Lord, and He answered me. He freed me from all my fears. Those who look to him for help will be radiant with joy; no shadow of shame will darken their faces" (Psalm 34:5 NLT).

P.S. You are loved.

TEN

From Graves to Gardens

The little grasses
Crack through stone
And they are green with life.
—Sylvia Plath—

JACK LONDON SAID, "THE MOST BEAUTIFUL STORIES ALWAYS START with wreckage."[1]

Present-day Southern Okinawa, the site of the island's bloodiest and most ruthless and gruesome fighting during WWII, testifies to the truth of London's observation. Time, natural forces, and soil (moved by caring hands, bulldozers, and excavators) have covered the carnage and silenced the suffering cries at the place American troops called Hacksaw Ridge. Today, on what the Japanese call the Maeda Escarpment, tidy pathways wind their way through huge rock formations and trees. Lush, green fields, grassy slopes, and rolling knolls, punctuated with war monuments—one is dedicated to Desmond Doss and his heroic rescue mission mentioned in the opening chapter —are as beautifully stunning as the vistas. If I were a betting person, I'd wager that not a single soldier on either side of the 1945 clash could have envisioned the plateau as a gloriously transformed, idyllic garden for visitors and curious historians. Who could have imagined that one day its tranquility would whisper to our souls to believe that something beautiful and peaceful can grow out of something painful, that from death, new life can burst through.

I'm hopeful that by now you are able to clearly recognize the freedom available to you. If you've reached this turning point and have experienced God's forgiveness, it's likely you feel relieved—confident there's no guilty verdict or punishment in your future. It's equally likely you feel the subtle, lingering power and tug of remnant shame. You might feel stuck as you struggle to forgive yourself. Your heart whispers peace, but your mind needs to catch up. I walked in those shoes, so may I suggest you do what I had to do? Allow, from the pen of the apostle Paul, the message of grace to settle the matter: "Now the decisive conclusion is this: in Christ, every bit of condemning evidence against us is canceled" (Romans 8:1 MSB). Another contemporary translation says it this way: "Those who enter into Christ's being-here-for-us no longer have to live under a continuous, low-lying black cloud. A new power is in operation" (Romans 8:1 MSG).

This is the reasonable diagnosis: You're at the place where your mind needs transformation and renewal. This is the reasonable prescription: Believe your case is closed. You have been released. Prison doors are behind you. Now it's important to speak over yourself what God says: *I have been declared not guilty. I am forgiven. I'm a new person. I am free. Therefore, there is now no condemnation for those who are in Christ Jesus.*[2] Repeat this often. Repeat it three or five times a day for weeks. Repeat it while standing on your head if necessary. Put it on index cards, on your mirror, on your dashboard. Speaking this truth out loud cancels every negative voice and thought that tries to hinder or restrain you. Speaking forth truth *will* penetrate your heart soon enough.

If, dear friend, you're at a crossroads where you're drawn to freedom but find yourself teetering on the side of oh-this-is-so-painful, this is okay. Be patient and kind to yourself. Pause. Exhale. Give yourself time to reflect on your life. There is no cookie-cutter formula to liberation. This is not science. It's not an open-and-shut five-step program. It's about turning down the volume of the world around you and allowing your inner heart to dialog with the living God. He never awakens a desire—forgiveness and healing included—that He cannot and will not satisfy in His own time and His own way.

Sometimes it's true that the more extended our confinement, the more prolonged our journey to confront our struggles and break free becomes. The whole process is entirely new and can seem scary. Maybe you're still held hostage to the choice you buried long ago or to the opinions of others. Maybe you still feel constricted by the power of secrecy. Maybe you're clenching your galaxy of doubts. Take comfort and allow the words of Ernest Hemingway to wash over you: "The world breaks everyone, and afterward, many are strong at the broken places."[3] Hold on. You're on your way to becoming stronger. You're an overcomer!

It bears repeating that the universal human experience of adversity and broken places is part of everyone's story. No one escapes it. No one is immune to hardships, setbacks, and failures. We all hit roadblocks. As it turns out—this is the *good news*—none of it has the final say. Not a single adverse experience gets the last word! Including your abortion(s). That event in your life is not the only chapter or the conclusion. It is not the whole story. It's only *part* of your history. In the final analysis, it turns out that the human condition is the essential condition for the divine to break in. I love what Frederick Buechner says about this good news:

> What is both Good and New about the Good News is … that if we will let him, God will actually bring about this unprecedented transformation of our hearts himself. …What is both Good and New about the Good News is the mad insistence that Jesus lives on among us … as the outlandish, holy, and invisible power of God working … in countless hidden ways to make even slobs like us loving and whole beyond anything we could conceivably pull off by ourselves.[4]

When God breaks in, the Author of tomorrow adjusts our stories to include a different if not a perfect ending. There are no exceptions. Every situation and every detail can be overcome, overruled, and overridden if you are willing to admit your need and change your mind about God. If you're willing to believe what He says about your worth and who you really are. If you're willing to ignore the approval or disapproval of family and friends. If you're willing to dismiss an unsympathetic media and a culture that values statistics and polls concerning what is morally legal and acceptable. If you're willing to trust that God enthusiastically longs to take every complicated mess and bring forth goodness, dignity, and honor. He longs to restore your beauty, value, and hope.

Hear the words of John the apostle: "The darkness is passing, and *the true light is already shining* (1 John 2:8 NIV, emphasis added)." Jesus calls Himself the Light of the World. His invitation to you is a signed, sealed, delivered promise of forgiveness and freedom forevermore—the ability to look at your future and say, "WOWZA!"

Wherever you find yourself on this journey to wholeness, listen for His voice as He calls you from darkness to light. See Him, arms stretched out wide, running toward you with extravagant, crazy love. He's welcoming you to step into the next chapter of your life, healed of every battle wound and liberated from every chain that binds you. The royal road to recovery starts with saying, "I'm sorry," and releasing your secrets. This is the way Frederick Beuchner describes it:

We are our secrets. They are the essence of what makes us ourselves. They are the rich loam out of which, for better or worse, grow the selves by which the world knows us. If we are ever to be free and whole, we must be free from their darkness and have their spell over us broken. If we are ever to see each other as we fully are, we must see by their light.

"Search me, O God, and know my heart!" cries out the great 139th Psalm, which is all about the hiding and baring of secrets. "Try me and know my thoughts ... for darkness is as light to thee." Even our darkness.

It is the secret prayer of us all.[5]

My greatest hope and expectation is that you will be open and responsive to what God is doing inside your heart. Resist the inclination to justify your past, deny your part, or deflect and blame others for what happened. Brennan Manning informs us, "Blame is a defensive substitute for an honest examination of life that seeks personal growth in failure and self-knowledge in mistakes."[6]

May I encourage you to flee secrecy and pursue His sweeping pardon? It's one of the marvels of God's grace that's already been won for you. Its healing power is magnificent. Accepting and opening it as a most glorious gift qualifies you to become part of the band of sisters who are becoming strong. Permitting Him to dig up what you buried and till the soil frees the space for a garden to be planted where your pain used to be.

I'm not an avid gardener per se, but I'm fond of gardens—from the formal, meticulously tended, symmetrical types in France to the verdant terrace variety in Peru. Here at home, I'm content with simple perennial gardens for several reasons. For starters, they require little effort, and they're easy to maintain. In early spring, as a nod to dormancy and darkness and winter's end, evidence of life and new growth peek through the earth. Soon, a charming floral ensemble creates a visual symphony of fresh textures, tones, and hues.

Lenten roses huddle and cuddle together in the cool of early spring. Dogwood and magnolia blooms herald warmer weather, azaleas are ablaze with blossoms, and purple bearded irises stand tall in all their royal splendor. In the summertime, gardenias fill the air with a pop of fragrance. The star performers, lacey hydrangeas of every color, bedazzle flower beds and pretty glass vases in indoor spaces with clusters of frilly layers and elegance. After the production, everything takes a bow and fades as temperatures cool again.

Gardens also serve as a powerful metaphor for humanity. After all, we got our start in paradise—in Eden, the scene of matchless and majestic beauty. In that garden and every one since, we find simplicity and intricacy. We find delicately folded petals and curled fronds waiting to release their potential. We find the great reward of delicious heirloom fruits and vegetables if we harvest before the critters do. As we tend to them, we find surprises like artfully spun webs or seasonal visitors like ruby-throated hummingbirds. We also encounter disappointment because things that are beyond our control—like the weather and June bugs—affect their performance.

Ultimately, gardens awaken us to the reality of the life cycle for all creation—plants, animals, and people. They prepare us to pause and ponder mortality and the mystery of life after death. Or a recycling center if we're not yet ready to wrestle with big questions involving our existence. In case you need a moment before we muse together about what it means to be revived, redeemed, and restored to life, it's probably the right time to tell you that my affinity for gardens stems from a childhood infatuation with flowers.

I drew them everywhere—on notebooks, on desks, and inside the closet where my brothers and I charted our growth. I was partial to wearing floral fabrics on pants, dresses, pajamas, and swimsuits. I have the vintage photos to prove it! I suppose I knew in an instinctive, intuitive way that flowers softened and eased the conflict, strife, and war that was part of my childhood—much like we drape and adorn coffins with garlands at funerals. The fixation grew into a kind of private obsession: I often dreamed about being a beautiful flower girl. For some ambitious reason, I was convinced I'd be the best flower girl for any bride in any wedding procession.

You might be as surprised as I was to learn that this tradition dates back to ancient Rome. The flower girl walked ahead of the bride, sprinkling her path with "grains and herbs representing the collective hope that the bride could also make little humans just like the ones tossing oatmeal, lest she be doomed to a life of barren dread."[7] In the Elizabethan era, probably because of a high infant mortality rate, the tradition of including children in the wedding party was a reflection of how the culture cherished and idealized childhood—they were seen as "symbols of hope and innocence."[8] Little humans. Hope and innocence.

Why I never got tapped to amble up the aisle, scattering petals ahead of one single, solitary bride in one single, solitary wedding, remained a personal conundrum. But I'm glad to report this was not lost on the cosmos. God was orchestrating something brand new in my life, and I wasn't even aware of it yet. The following is a trustworthy account demonstrating how He is intimately acquainted with and involved in *every* detail of our lives. As a missionary friend often points out, He's always stacking up evidence of His goodness.

It just so happened that between college graduation and the birth of my first child, one special colleague and friend named Wynne affectionately called me "Hortense." She gave no reason. At first, I privately wondered if she called me Hortense because—I don't know —maybe she secretly thought I looked like a horse. She was wise, had a big personality, and a gift for showering joy over all things professional and personal, so it didn't take long to embrace the nickname and respond to it as if it were a badge of honor. What's noteworthy is that whenever I heard "Hortense!" or "Hello, Hortense!" or "Good-bye, Hortense!" two things happened. I'd giggle every time, and at some deep level, I would feel greater and grander, more colorful and playful.

This might seem frivolous, but as Eugene H. Peterson describes,

The personal name is the most important part of speech in our language. Names not only address what we are, the irreplaceably human, they also anticipate what we become. Names call us to become who we will be. A lifetime of growth and development is announced by a name. Names mean something. A personal name designates what is irreducibly personal; it also calls us to become what we are not yet. … The meaning of a name is not in the dictionary, not in the unconscious, not in the size of the lettering. It is in relationship—with

God. Naming is a way of hoping. We name a child after someone or some quality that we hope he or she will become—a saint, a hero, an admired ancestor. … Naming is not a whim; it's a lever of hope against the future. …No child is just a child. Each is a creature in whom God intends to do something glorious and great. A personal name is our passport into reality. It is also our continuing orientation into reality."[9]

The import of Wynne's endearing nickname surfaced long after she moved and life forced us to take different paths. In fact, it wasn't until I was writing an early chapter for this book—specifically the details about not being named until three days after my birth—that I was able to connect the dots. On that particular day, I was moved to research the meaning of my first and middle names, but I uncovered so much more. I was riveted by the discovery that the fullness of their meanings expanded beyond what I had always been told.

The names of our three children—the choice and the significance of each were important to us—were also more pregnant with meaning than Prince Charming and I realized. What happened next might appear fabricated or even farfetched, but please believe every word is true.

The idea surfaced to look up my old nickname. A quick search revealed that Hortense, of French and Latin origin, means "garden." My heart smiled.

Over the next few weeks or so, two more events convinced me I was in the midst of something divinely orchestrated. While out for a walk one spring morning, I passed the house my parents rented when I was seven weeks old. A gentleman was pruning roses at the edge of his lawn, so I approached him and introduced myself. I explained my connection to the home—that I lived there as a baby. He cast a wide smile, extended his hand, and introduced himself as Mr. Gardner, the owner. *Gardner! That word again!*

Later that week, I was reading an account of the crucifixion of Jesus, and I noticed a particular verse I didn't recall seeing before. At least it hadn't caused my heart to flutter like it did that day when it skipped and hopped off the page! In his recorded account of Jesus's death, the apostle John notes, "In the place where Jesus was crucified, *there was a garden*" (John 19:41 NIV, emphasis added). Every part of me stood at attention! The word was popping up everywhere. *Is this a fluke? Serendipity? A treasure hunt?* Frederick Buechner defines the magnitude of the convergence:

> I believe that people laugh at coincidence as a way of relegating it to the realm of the absurd and of therefore not having to take seriously the possibility that there is a lot more going on in our lives than we either know or care to know. Who can say what it is that's going on, but I suspect that part of it, anyway, is that every once and so often we hear a whisper from the wings that goes something like this: "You've turned up in the right place at the right time. You're doing fine. Don't ever think you've been forgotten.[10]

Coincidence? God wink? Whatever you want to call it, in that dazzling, quiet morning instant, I received an inner knowing—a motherlode of insight. There had been a lot more going on in my life than I ever realized, and it was still playing out in real time! Neither my name, Prince Charming's name, nor the names of our children had been given on a whim. All of our names were hope-filled and hinted at destiny. Including Hortense! Strange as it may sound, the nickname, given to me as I approached the threshold of motherhood, effectively awakened my spiritual eyes and increased my physical awareness. As Hanna Rion says, "The greatest gift of the garden is the restoration of the five senses."[11]

As I stared in the rearview mirror, I realized Hortense provided confirmation that God had been speaking and working in and throughout my entire life. He hadn't forgotten or abandoned me. He never called it quits between us. Ever! He was always near. His eyes were on me before I was born. He presided over me as an unnamed baby when the cosmic battle for my life was set in motion, when my mother was solo and my father was halfway around the world watching Pakistani snake charmers. He called me by name and spoke to me when I felt rejected as a young girl. He was by my side through all the complexities and when I navigated—rudderless and anchorless—in the hard places and testing grounds. He saw me even when I felt hidden.

He watched as I allowed the build-up of anger and resentment. He witnessed all the temptations, the rebellion, and the decisions that caused me to go sideways and tailspin. He continued to walk with me through my wilderness years. In seasons of despondency, despair, and delay, the Master Gardener continued tilling the soil. He was preparing to break new ground with the gift of three beautiful, healthy children. The significance of each of their names became clear in the fullness of time. For example, while writing this book, I learned the Hebrew meaning of our oldest child's name: "God has given." Precisely! He gave! God gave more generously than what I took. His divine, threefold kindness led to the radical awakening of my body, soul, and spirit.

This new and unexpected evidence settled the guess that He had walked with me on the mercy road. He had seen me in the separation from my dad, my hurts, feelings of being unloved, and struggles with emotional abandonment and rejection. He shared in the sorrow over my failures—and all the physical, emotional, and spiritual consequences. He presided over every sigh, ache, doubt, every miscarriage, and every other pain and loss in my life. Such knowledge caused my heart to echo words of the psalmist, "You keep track of all my sorrows. You have collected all my tears in your bottle. You have recorded each one in your book" (Psalm 56:8 NLT). What a crystal clear reminder that in the pitch and yaw and roll of life, He holds us. The mercy of God sustains us.

There's more! I believe Hortense was given in the past for a future purpose—to rouse me to the unrelenting grace of God. He illuminated points where He showered me with His goodness—one blessing after another—from the title of "Little Miss Sea Orbit" and my family and childhood to the homecoming crown before I was wounded in the battle. I could identify grace at work in every area—including my marriage with Prince Charming, each addition to our family, and beyond. He presided over every wise choice, every giggle, every cause for celebration, and every joy. It was obvious my imagination had tricked me; He wasn't waiting for the perfect time to send down a deadly lightning bolt. He wasn't waiting for me to clean and polish up my life for Him, either. Nobody can do that. All along He was holding the door open for a redemptive purpose. He was waiting for me to respond, to consent to being loved by Him, and to enter into a new and repurposed life.

In those early morning hours in sweet daughter's bedroom, He saw the real me—the me He created and the me who would resurface after He put me in right standing with Him. When my internal narrative insisted my life, at least in part, was in ruins, He gave me a heightened awareness of His presence and love. He enabled me to respond decisively and experience His grace. I was catapulted into a greater reality. No more mediocrity. No more embracing the inferior. I began, unhindered and with His help, to live into the meaning of my given name. "Divine," "shining one," "gift," and "song" became a source of strength and confidence.

The prophet Isaiah beautifully describes how our lives are turned around when God frees us, binds up our broken hearts, and comforts us: "He bestows on us a crown of beauty instead of ashes, the oil of gladness instead of mourning, and a garment of praise instead of a spirit of despair" (Isaiah 61:3 NIV).

God masterfully weaves together every thread as He creates a beautiful tapestry.

The same is true for you, my friend. A thousand times ten thousand times. Will you trust that God is wooing you, too, to believe that He has always been *for* you? Will you trust that He has been cheering you *forth* through all the harmonies and disharmonies? Even now, He continues to patiently and powerfully work on your behalf to free you from the works of the chief antagonist, your nemesis. The real-life adversary represented by the villain Christof in *The Truman Show*. He is the archenemy who works tirelessly to get you to think, say, and do things that sully, stain, tarnish, and mar your true identity as an image bearer of God. The devil is real. He's the one who wars against your soul, deceives you, and tempts you to doubt that you're a candidate for a clean slate and adoption as a dearly loved child of God.

Friend, please hear me! God is committed to pursuing you. Nothing you've done—not a single choice—has disqualified you from His grace. Your very life and every breath are blessings from Him. He wants to give you a heightened awareness of His love for you. He sees the beauty in you that you're unable to see. He is crazy about you!

You have heard it said—and maybe you've said this yourself—that everything works for good. I think we're conditioned from a young age to secretly cross our fingers behind our back and utter this cliche with a pie-in-the-sky hope that everything will turn out alright. At this point, a truer version rooted in and overflowing with confident hope is worth memorizing: "And we know that in all things God works *for the good of those who love Him* (emphasis added), who have been called according to his purpose" (Romans 8:28 ESV). The Passion Translation expresses it this way, "So we are convinced that every detail of our lives is continually woven together to fit into God's perfect plan of bringing good into our lives, for we are his lovers who have been called to fulfill his designed purpose" (Romans 8:28). Wintley Phipps says it like this, "It is in the quiet crucible of your personal private sufferings that your noblest dreams are born and God's greatest gifts are given in compensation for what you've been through."[12]

George Washington Carver once said, "Where there is no vision, there is no hope."[13] Vision matters. Your vision for your life matters a lot. I want to encourage you right now to take time to visualize yourself as God sees you—flawless and without defect. Be filled with hope. Can you picture yourself free of emotional distress? Free of paralyzing humiliation? Free of all guilts, low-grade depressions, fear, and punishment?

Inhale. Can you feel and see yourself radiating abundant joy? Can you imagine yourself as a beautiful, golden thread in His colorful tapestry? Can you picture your life as His trophy? His masterpiece?

Can you envision yourself, to borrow the words of King Solomon, "clothed in strength and dignity, smiling at the days to come?"[14] Permit the words of the Psalmist to penetrate even your bones, "I sought the LORD, and he answered me; He delivered me from all my fears. Those who look to Him are radiant; their faces are never covered with shame" (Psalm 34:4–5 NIV).

Now exhale.

This, my friend, is where God wants to bring you. At this point in our journey, I bid you to look to Him and believe Him. What do you have to lose? He's saying, "Give Me a chance to bless you, to come through for you." Nobody else offers or guarantees permanent change. Nobody else offers or guarantees a cure. Nobody else offers or guarantees complete peace, healing, and wholeness. Only God can recover us from the ruins of a degrading exile. He alone is the source of our liberation and lasting hope. Everything hinges on what He has done for us.

The garden is the springboard that points us to the reason why.

You may remember my mention of a garden in the place where Jesus was crucified. Before we address its importance and connect the dots, I need to shed light on His crucifixion, a savage and ghastly execution. In every way it was like the horror on Hacksaw Ridge—gruesome, gut-churning, bloody. It was equally real. It was equally historic. Its scope, however, far exceeded that single WWII battle and every battle in every other war and world war that has ever been fought. In the purest sense, it was and will forever be *THE* world's first great war—one man's fight for the world.

Make no mistake, though, His death on a cross had been part of the master war plan for millennia. The wise general and mastermind, God Himself, was its strategist. For He so loved the world—you, me, and everyone else since the dawn of time—that He freely gave His one and only Son to live among us. To lift our heads. To do good to all. To heal our brokenness. To point us to the extravagant care, compassion, and love of the Father.

The crazy part? Jesus willingly agreed to be sent on the mission and to wear our skin—our human uniform. He's not a religious feature. He's relevant. During His short, thirty-three years on earth, He was tempted and provoked in every way known to man. And yet He lived a perfect, sinless life. In other words, unlike us, He did everything right, every time, and for all the right reasons. There was no spot on His birth record or blemish on His life record. He didn't need forgiveness like we do. But He laid a freeway for it for you and me.

His reward? He became the scorn of us mere men and women. The climax of the war against Him—the epitome of injustice—gained momentum when the political and religious powers of His day exchanged His life for that of a notorious murderer and prisoner. Then they threw Him to the proverbial wolves. He suffered in unimaginable ways. He was led to a whipping post where He was scourged by soldiers. His ravaged body, beaten and ripped beyond recognition, was then nailed to a cross on a hill outside the city. As He hung there, suspended between heaven and earth, breathing His final breaths, all the weight of our wrongs—*my choice, your choice,* and all the unintended consequences of pain, humiliation, stigma, abandonment, shame, guilt, and grief—was placed on Him.

The mind bending part of all this is that it was *His choice* to die this substitutionary death to buy us back for His Father. His life in exchange for ours. In other words, when He was on the cross, rejected by man and seemingly rejected by heaven, the Son of God took on Himself the punishment that all of humankind earned because of our folly, our rebellion, our waywardness, and our self-willed, revolting decisions. Yes, He chose to pay the penalty even for us so-called "abortion persons." Love, in the person of Jesus, endured all the wrath and fury and hell we deserve.

Before His final breath, He pronounced forgiveness. For me. For you. For everyone who would look to Him and believe He died to save us, free us, and heal us—from our worst deeds, from ourselves, and from eternal death. Trust me, His forgiveness is not normal. It is out of this world! In the strongest terms, for our sake, God put the wrong on Him who never did anything wrong so we could be made right with God forever—as if we never slipped up and never got it wrong.[15]

Brennan Manning highlights the outcome of the exchange this way: "If we follow the instinct that a healer has to know by experience the pain he or she heals, we better understand why there's only one healer —Jesus. Only someone who has known our agony and suffering could by his coming transform that agony into peace. The One who comes to heal has been there and shared every hurt known to humankind."[16]

Before sunset, Jesus's dead body was taken from the cross and laid inside a tomb. A garden tomb. No one—including His followers who felt dejected, demoralized, and crushed—could have fathomed anything beautiful springing from the day's unspeakably monstrous and loathsome experience.

But God!

In three days—this is the fun part—the world was treated to the most unnatural yet most spectacular end-of-story twist. The breathtaking culmination of the master plan exceeded any fable or fairytale the human mind can possibly conceive, concoct, or cook up. It was so absolutely genius that it took even the enemy of our souls by surprise. Suffice it to say death could not hold down the perfectly-lived life of God's Son. And since His life was death-proof, Jesus triumphantly rose to life from the grave.

Today, He stands before our battlefield. He stands before every pit and trench and self-dug grave and calls us to exit the darkness of half living. He entreats us to shed our guilty conscience by agreeing with Him that abortion doesn't fit with who we are. To confess that it has hindered inner peace and joy in our hearts and has prevented us from stepping into authentic tranquility and serenity. Face to face, He quietly whispers that His story can be your story. Yes, you, too, can be raised from the ruins victorious.

Darkness is powerless to stop His light from breaking through. Just as the sun pierces through dark soil to reach the perennial that's been stunted and silenced after a harsh, cold winter, His light shines on you. He offers you redemption and restoration and fresh, green purpose. He promises you new life so you can live out the rest of your beautiful life in full bloom!

Listen to His voice: "Are you tired? Worn out? … Come to me. Get away with me and you'll recover your life. I'll show you how to take a real rest. Walk with me and work with me—watch how I do it. Learn the unforced rhythms of grace. I won't lay anything heavy or ill-fitting on you. Keep company with me, and you'll learn to live freely and lightly" (Matthew 11:28–30 MSG).

God is calling you by name. Welcome the Master Gardener who will turn your grave into a garden.

AN INVITATION

In the labyrinth of life, where paths often twist and turn, there lies a profound truth, simple yet profound. God says to you, "You will seek me and find Me when you search for Me with all your heart" (Jeremiah 29:13 NASB). This isn't just a promise; it's a divine assurance. It's an invitation to embark on the most rewarding quest you'll ever undertake—the quest to seek and find God.

The promise of God's presence is not a riddle wrapped in a mystery. It's an open declaration—a standing invitation echoing through time and space. God is not hiding. He's waiting. His heart's desire is for your heart to turn toward Him and for your soul to tune into His frequency. He is waiting for you to earnestly seek Him.

Trust and believe God will make a difference in your life today. He is there, waiting to be found in the multitude of your life's moments. But know this: Seeking God is not a passive endeavor. It is an active pursuit that demands dedication, intentionality, and a heart open to transformation. Pursuing God is about making space for Him in the crowded rooms of your mind and heart. It's about tuning your ears to His voice amid the complexity of life's demands. It's about seeking His will for your decisions, His wisdom in your confusion, and His peace in every circumstance.

In this journey, be reassured. God's arm is not too short to save. His ear is not too dull to hear. He is closer than you think and more willing to reveal Himself than you can imagine. As dawn dispels darkness, God's presence illuminates shadows of uncertainty and doubt. "Draw near to God, and He will draw near to you" (James 4:8 ESV).

P.S. You are loved!

Postscript

Miracles happen because of the willingness
to open the door into your pain.
Open your ears and your eyes
to the elusive, invisible, silent presence of healing,
of the power of God to heal, which moves as quietly,
and undramatically, as the wind moves.
—Frederick Beuchner—

One of my favorite authors offers such comforting words: "I'm inclined to believe that God's chief purpose in giving us memory is to enable us to go back in time so that if we didn't play those roles right the first time round, we can still have another go at it now. We cannot undo our old mistakes or their consequences any more than we can erase old wounds that we have both suffered and inflicted, but through the power that memory gives us of thinking, feeling, imagining our way back through time, we can at long last finally finish with the past in the sense of removing its power to hurt us and other people and to stunt our growth as human beings."[1]

Friend, just as your journey to enslavement on the battlefield was unique, so, too, will be your journey to freedom. It might be downright intimidating to think you're on your own as you pivot decisively into a time of self-reflection, self-examination, and a journey through memories and backstories. But as you take one step backward in preparation for a giant leap forward, be strengthened by two simple and important truths. First, you are *not* alone on this path to forgiveness and healing—God is at your side. I've heard Bill Johnson say, "It is in the heart and history of God to bring healing when there has been a failing and a falling." God has a habit of bringing healing and restoration, work only He can do. Have faith that with Him *all* will be well. You're important to Him. His care and love for you is way deeper, wider, higher, longer and greater than you can imagine. He's wild about you!

Second, memory is a *good* thing. You've been wired and gifted with it by design. Traveling back through doors into fearful, hurtful, and dark places may be a painful, fiery ordeal, but I promise you will be given the strength to go there. You will find God there too. I guarantee you will return to the light with an inner peace that surpasses all understanding, and you won't even smell like smoke. Please trust me, it's a sure path. By all means, and if necessary, do it afraid!

Finally, for anyone who might still be stuck in doubt and unbelief, I want to encourage you to act and not hesitate concerning the information you now have. Listen carefully to Dr. Bernard Nathanson, the OB-GYN who had over 75,000 encounters with abortion, as he whispers through his memoir that sits on a shelf in my personal library: "The cost of believing in God is minimal; the consequences of doubt may be significant."[2]

God liberated Dr. Nathanson from chains and gave him new life, too. If He did it for us, He will do the same for you. He's rousing you to pull you into His embrace. Expect Him to show you that you were born for so much more. The rest of your life can be the best of your life!

Helpful Resources

We've touched on one of the most difficult and complex issues of our lifetime. I encourage you to continue seeking additional recovery and healing you may need. Thankfully, there is a compassionate community of counselors and organizations providing a continuum of care after abortion. While not exhaustive, I'm including a list of online resources and groups offering confidential help. Each can equip and empower you for the present and point you to a future of freedom and lasting hope. A short reading list is included too.

FOR FURTHER HELP:

— **AbortionHealing.org**
(703) 770-8000

— **AfterAbortion.org**

— **EnteringCanaan.com**

— **American Association of Pro-Life OBGYNs:**
Offers healing tips and resources.
aaplog.org/post-abortion-healing/

— **EnteringCanaan.com**

— **Healing Hearts Ministries International:**
HealingHearts.org

— **Human Life International:**
hli.org

— **NationalHelpline.org**
(866) 482-5433

— **OperationOutcry.org**

— **OptionLine.org**
(800) 712-4357

— **Physicians For Life:**
Offers resources for recovery.
PhysiciansForLife.org

— **Rachel's Vineyard:**
Offers healing retreats.
RachelsVineyard.org
(877) 467-3463

— **Silent No More Awareness:**
Offers a list of national and international
support and recovery groups.
SilentNoMoreAwareness.org

— **SupportAfterAbortion.com**
(844) 289-HOPE (4673)

— **And Then There Were None:**
Offers counsel and care unique
to former abortion clinic workers.
AbortionWorker.com

— **We Care Experts:**
Provides accurate, unbiased
information on abortion and health.
WeCareExperts.org

FOR FURTHER SUPPORT & STUDY:

— *Surrendering Your Secret: Healing the Heartbreak of
Abortion*, Pat Layton (Nashville: Serendipity House
Publishing, 2007).

— *Transforming Your Story: A Path to Healing After
Abortion*, Wendy Giancola (Washington, DC: Capitol
Hill Pregnancy Center, 2018).

— *The Four Steps to Healing*, Debbie McDaniel, M.A. LPC
and Martha Shuping, M.D. (Tabor Garden Press, 2007).

NEW BEGINNINGS:

— *Basic Christianity*, John R.W. Stott (Grand Rapids: Inter-
Varsity, 1958).

— *How to Begin the Christian Life*, George Sweeting
(Chicago: Moody Publishers, 1993).

— *I'll Hold You in Heaven: Healing and Hope for the Parent Who Has Lost a Child through Miscarriage, Stillbirth, Abortion, or Early Infant Death*, Jack Hayford (Ventura: Regal Books, 1986).

— *Right with God*, John Blanchard (Edinburgh, United Kingdom: Banner of Truth, 1996).

Acknowledgments

I am eternally grateful to those who inspired and encouraged me as I wrote *She Smiles at the Days to Come*. What seemed insurmountable yesterday is a reality today. And now begins the real work of sharing the message of peace and restoration for women who have experienced the unfreedom of abortion. Each one is precious and unique. Each one matters.

No combination of words can accurately express my gratitude to or for the Messenger Books Publishing family. Simply put, your sincere, do-all-things-with-excellence partnership with aspiring authors is second to none. A big merci beaucoup to Teresa and Jeremiah Yancy, Brian Simmons, Patricia King, David Sluka, and the amazing staff behind the scenes. Your friendship, teaching, coaching, accessibility, strengthening prayers, and heartfelt support of my message are extraordinary. There's a special reward awaiting you.

To Allen, my Prince Charming and best friend. You loved me well in the light of my darkest confession. You cheered for me—untiringly —whether I was in the thick of writing or sidelined by distractions. You celebrated and spurred me on. You truly are the quintessential supportive husband and father. You are a gift of great value. I love you.

To our children Nathan (Annie), Catherine, and David. Each of you is a priceless, matchless treasure. This mama llama loves you and honors you with all my heart. Your grace, maturity, and affirmation before and during my writing project are more than appreciated. Take courage, stand firm, and be amazed as every good purpose and plan for your lives unfold.

To my mother and my late father. I love you. How I wish I hadn't believed the lie that I was alone in my darkest hour. Thank you for giving me grace when I shared my story with you, for affirming me, and for always loving me. God blessed me with you, Mark, Matthew, and our entire extended family.

Many thanks to LaTan Murphy and Jill Steele, my writing conference friends and sisters who love to laugh. You believed in me and my message and inspired me to press forward.

Mountains of gratitude for my mentor and friend Diana DeBoe and the Rev. Dr. Jayce O'Neal. I know your review of my manuscript and vision for the reader were driven by love.

To Karissa, the beautiful and talented woman behind the images and creative expression of all-things social media and more. I'm amazed by and grateful for you.

To my circle of valued and faithful friends—Helene, Bethany, Susan, Gina, Kathy, Jerri, Maryrose, Deb, Jana, Ruthie, Nancy, Deborah, Nancy, Christine, and the Monday morning prayer group. I couldn't have reached the finish line without your listening ears, life-giving words, and caring hearts. Thank you for gifting me with your love, grace, laughter, and joy along the way.

I salute the Rev. Coleman and Susan Tyler for inviting Georgette Forney to speak life and minister to the wounded.

My deepest thanks and highest esteem go to Georgette Forney. Your courage to share your story inspires others. Your passion to pursue, reach, and love the burdened and brokenhearted has changed countless lives. I want to be like you.

A huge thank you goes to Dr. Linda Mintle who shared time, wisdom, and the truth of Romans 8:1 with me. Remnant threads of shame were torn apart in the quaint little chapel that morning.

Finally, thank You for Your goodness, Jesus. The height, length, and width of Your great love qualified me to walk from shame into Your glorious light. This is for You.

About the Author

Diane is a passionate student of American culture and issues that shape our nation's character. She is a voice of hope for those who have experienced pregnancy loss and an advocate for their freedom, healing, and wholeness. Following college and a brief career in banking and real estate, she devoted herself wholeheartedly to family life. She has volunteered with and served on the board of non-profit, non-partisan public policy organizations. Diane and her husband, Allen, live in Virginia near their amazing children. They enjoy family surf trips and travel on international roads.

Notes

BEFORE WE BEGIN

1. Carmine Gallo, *The Storyteller's Secret: From Ted Speakers to Business Legends, Why Some Ideas Catch on and Others Don't* (New York, NY: St. Martin's Press, 2016), 224.
2. Henry J. M. Nouwen, *Life of the Beloved: Spiritual Living in a Secular World* (Chicago, IL: The Crossroad Publishing Co, 1992), 21, 23.
3. David C. Reardon, *The Jericho Plan: Breaking Down the Walls Which Prevent Post-Abortion Healing* (Springfield, IL: Acorn Books, 1996), 59.
4. Harper Lee, *To Kill a Mockingbird* (New York, NY: Harper Perennial Modern Classics, 2006), 36.
5. Frederick Buechner, *Wishful Thinking: A Seeker's ABC* (San Francisco, CA: HarperSanFrancisco, 1993), 18.
6. Frederick Buechner, "Cripples All of Us," Frederick Buechner, March 24, 2021, https://www.frederickbuechner.com/.

1. FOR THE SAKE OF ONE

1. Gibson, Mel, dir. *Hacksaw Ridge* (Santa Monica, CA: Summit Entertainment, 2016), tv.apple.com.
2. *Hacksaw Ridge,* 1:00:12-1:00:40.
3. *Hacksaw Ridge,* 1:48:50-1:51:51.
4. Kate Clifford Larson, *Harriet Tubman Portrait of an American Hero* (New York, NY: Random House, 2003), 88.
5. Anne Lamott, *Bird by Bird: Some Instruction on Writing and Life* (New York, NY: Random House, 1994), 193.
6. Miriam Grossman, *Unprotected: A Campus Psychiatrist Reveals How Political Correctness in Her Profession Endangers Every Student* (New York, NY: Sentinel, a member of Penguin Group (USA) Inc., 2007), 103.
7. Lisa Rowe, "Helping People in the Church Heal After Abortion," *Life SUMMIT 2024* (lecture, Falls Church, VA, January 20, 2024).
8. Brennan Manning, *The Ragamuffin Gospel* (New York, NY: Penguin Random House, 2005), 45.
9. Manning, *The Ragamuffin Gospel*, 175.
10. Lamott, *Bird by Bird*, 200.
11. Lasseter, John, dir. *Toy Story* (Emeryville, CA, Disney/Pixar, 1995), tv.apple.com.
12. *Toy Story,* 11:07-11:16.
13. Brennan Manning, *The Wisdom of Tenderness: What Happens When God's Fierce Mercy Transforms Our Lives* (New York, NY: HarperSanFrancisco, 2004), 49-51.

2. NO STRANGER TO WAR

1. Sydney Smith, Saba Holland Holland, and Sarah Austin, *A Memoir of the Reverend Sydney Smith*, vol. 1, 2 vols. (New York: Harper, 1855), 9.
2. Carmine Gallo, *The Storyteller's Secret: From Ted Speakers to Business Legends, Why Some Ideas Catch on and Others Don't* (New York, NY: St. Martin's Press, 2016), 146-147.
3. John Newton, *Thoughts upon the African Slave Trade* (LaVergne, TN: Gale Ecco, Print Editions, 2010), 1-2.
4. John Newton, *Thoughts upon the African Slave Trade* (LaVergne, TN: Gale Ecco, Print Editions, 2010), 1-2.
5. Frederick Buechner, *A Crazy, Holy Grace: The Healing Power of Pain and Memory* (Grand Rapids, MI: Zondervan, 2017), 130.
6. Buechner, *A Crazy, Holy Grace,* 31.
7. Buechner, *A Crazy, Holy Grace*, 37.
8. Eugene H. Peterson, *Run with the Horses: The Quest for Life at Its Best* (Lisle, IL: InterVarsity Press, 2009), 24.
9. Carmine Gallo, *The Storyteller's Secret: From Ted Speakers to Business Legends, Why Some Ideas Catch on and Others Don't* (New York, NY: St. Martin's Press, 2016), 34, 36.

3. THE CROWNING AND THE CRISIS

1. Henry Cloud, *Changes That Heal: How to Understand Your Past to Ensure a Healthier Future* (Grand Rapids, MI: Zondervan Publishing House, 1992), 309.
2. Shyer, Charles, dir. *Father of the Bride* (Burbank, CA, Touchstone Pictures, 1991), tv.apple.com, 3:30-4:19.
3. Henry Cloud, *Changes That Heal: How to Understand Your Past to Ensure a Healthier Future* (Grand Rapids, MI: Zondervan Publishing House, 1992), 309.

4. POISED BETWEEN PEACE AND WAR

1. Brest, Martin, dir. *Scent of a Woman* (Universal City, CA, Universal Pictures, 1992), tv.apple.com.
2. *Scent of a Woman,* 2:24:29-2:25:09.
3. Christine Caine, *Undaunted* (Grand Rapids, MI: Zondervan, 2019), 44.
4. Henry David Thoreau Quotes. BrainyQuote.com, BrainyMedia Inc, 2023. https://www.brainyquote.com/quotes/henry_david_thoreau_106041, accessed September 11, 2023.
5. M. Scott Peck, *The Road Less Traveled: A New Psychology of Love, Traditional Values and Spiritual Growth* (New York, NY: Simon & Schuster, 1978), 23-24.
6. Karin Barbito, Melinda Means, and Lisa Rowe, *Unraveled Roots: Exposing the Hidden Causes of Damaging Behaviors* (United States: Martin Publishing Services, 2020), 17-19.
7. Dr. Seuss, *Oh, the Places You Will Go* (New York, NY: Random House, 1990), 4-5.

8. Brennan Manning, *The Ragamuffin Gospel* (New York, NY: Penguin Random House, 2005), 152.

9. Dr. Seuss, *Horton Hears a Who!* (New York: Random House, 1954), 6.

10. Tom Sawyer (*Adventures of Huckleberry Finn*) https://bookroo.com/quotes/tom-sawyer.

11. M. Scott Peck, *Glimpses of the Devil: A Psychiatrist's Personal Accounts of Possession, Exorcism, and Redemption* (New York, NY: Simon and Schuster, 2005), 222.

12. Theresa Karminski Burke and David C. Reardon, *Forbidden Grief: The Unspoken Pain of Abortion* (Springfield, IL: Acorn Books, 2002), 223.

13. Burke and Reardon, *Forbidden Grief,* 223.

14. Burke and Reardon, *Forbidden Grief,* 225.

15. Jeanette Vought, *Post-Abortion Trauma: 9 Steps to Recovery* (Grand Rapids, MI: Zondervan, 1991), 17.

16. *Scent of a Woman,* 2:23:13-2:23:23.

17. Karin Barbito, Melinda Means, and Lisa Rowe, *Unraveled Roots: Exposing the Hidden Causes of Damaging Behaviors* (United States: Martin Publishing Services, 2020), 15.

5. THE WILDERNESS

1. Wikipedia contributors, "Ten Commandments," *Wikipedia, The Free Encyclopedia,* https://en.wikipedia.org/w/index.php?title=Ten_Commandments&oldid=1157954150 (accessed June 1, 2023).

2. *The Ten Commandments,* film (United States: Paramount Pictures, 1956).

3. Eugene H. Peterson, *Leap over a Wall: Earthy Spirituality for Everyday Christians* (New York, NY: HarperOne an imprint of Harper Collins Publishers, 1998), 92.

4. David C. Reardon, *The Jericho Plan: Breaking down the Walls Which Prevent Post-Abortion Healing* (Springfield, IL: Acorn Books, 1996), 22.

5. Burke and Reardon, *Forbidden Grief,* 242.

6. Jack London, *The Call of the Wild* (United States: Elegant Ebooks, 1903), 15, https://www.ibiblio.org/ebooks/London/Call%20of%20Wild.pdf.

7. Charles Dickens, *Cricket on the Hearth: We Forge the Chains We Wear in Life* (S.l.: A Word To The Wise, 2013), subtitle.

8. Nathaniel Hawthorne, *The Scarlet Letter* (Mineola, NY: Dover Publications, 1994), 37.

9. Michel de Montaigne, *Les Essais (1595) [The Essays], Book III* (London, England: Penguin Classics, 1994).

10. Warren Hern. *Abortion Practice* (Philadelphia, PA:J.B. Lippincott Company, 1990), 101-103.

11. "The Medical Effects of Induced Abortion," Planned Parenthood, February 2014, https://www.plannedparenthood.org/uploads/filer_public/0c/9a/0c9a91c0-3e94-48d8-b110-374da1275df8/abortion_emotional_effects.pdf, 1-3.

12. Grossman, *Unprotected,* 84-89.

13. Diana Greene Foster, *The Turnaway Study Ten Years, a Thousand Women, and the Consequences of Having--or Being Denied--an Abortion* (New York, NY: Scribner, 2021), 7.

14. "Concerned Citizens Presents: The Turnaway Study Author Diana Green Foster on the Effects of Abortion," YouTube, March 9, 2022, https://www.youtube.com/.

15. "Abortion Statistics: United States Data and Trends," National Right to Life, January 2022, https://nrlc.org/uploads/factsheets//FS01AbortionintheUS.pdf, 1.

16. Peterson, *Run with the Horses*, 43.

17. Burke and Reardon, *Forbidden Grief*, 29.

18. Jodi Picoult, *Vanishing Acts* (New York, NY: Simon & Schuster, 2007), 425.

19. "Our Purpose," Support After Abortion, 2024, https://supportafterabortion.com/about/our-purpose.

20. Peterson, *Leap over a Wall*, 74.

21. Peterson, *Run with the Horses*, 154.

6. RESCUE BEGINS

1. Weir, Peter, dir. *The Truman Show* (Los Angeles, CA: Paramount Pictures, 1998), tv.apple.com.

2. Weir, *The Truman Show*, 29:27-29:36.

3. Marcus Aurelius, *Meditations*, GoodReads.com. https://www.goodreads.com/quotes/73581-if-someone-is-able-to-show-me-that-what-i

4. Burke and Reardon, *Forbidden Grief*, 60.

5. Buechner, *A Crazy, Holy Grace*, 43.

6. Jackie Kendall, *Free Yourself to Love: The Liberating Power of Forgiveness* (New York, NY: Faith Words, 2009), 21.

7. See Luke 8:1.

8. Grossman, *Unprotected*, 81-82.

9. Kim Ketola, *Cradle My Heart: Finding God's Love after Abortion* (Grand Rapids, MI: Kregel Publications, 2012), 21.

10. Burke and Reardon, *Forbidden Grief*, 29.

11. Pat Layton, *Surrendering the Secret: Healing the Heartbreak of Abortion* (Nashville, TN: Serendipity House, 2007), 35.

12. Coleman McCarthy, "The Real Anguish of Abortions," *Washington Post*, February 15, 1989.

13. Burke and Reardon, *Forbidden Grief*, 33.

14. Seuss, *Oh, the Places*, 18-19.

15. Dan B. Allender and Larry Crabb, *The Wounded Heart: Hope for Adult Victims of Childhood Sexual Abuse* (Colorado Springs, CO: NavPress, 2018), 153.

16. Max Lucado, *Anxious for Nothing: Finding Calm in a Chaotic World* (Nashville: Thomas Nelson, 2017), 37.

17. Manning, *The Ragamuffin Gospel*, 127.

18. The Pretenders. (1982). Back on the Chain Gang [CD]. On *Learning to Crawl*. AIR Studios, London; Chris Thomas.

19. Ann Patchett and Chip Kidd, *What Now?* (New York, NY: Harper Collins, 2008), 77-78.

7. RUNNING AWAY

1. Walker Percy, *The Moviegoer* (New York, NY: Avon Books, 1980), 18.
2. Charles Colson, with Ellen Santilli Vaughn, "Living in the New Dark Ages," *Christianity Today* (October 20, 1989), 30-31
3. Peterson, *Run with the Horses*, 146.
4. Dr. Seuss, *Did I Ever Tell You How Lucky You Are?* (New York: Random House, 2004), 20.
5. Bernard N. Nathanson, *The Hand of God: A Journey from Death to Life by the Abortion Doctor Who Changed His Mind* (Washington, D.C.: Regnery Publishing, 1996), 4-5, 55.
6. David Kupelian, *The Marketing of Evil: How Radicals, Elitists, and Pseudo-Experts Sell US Corruption Disguised as Freedom* (Nashville, Tenn: WND Books, 2005), 192-194.
7. Carol Everett and Gary McCaleb, "Interview with Carol Everett," The Portal to Texas History, July 9, 2017, https://texashistory.unt.edu/ark:/67531/metapth864049/.
8. Norma McCorvey and Gary Thomas, *Won by Love: Norma McCorvey, Jane Roe of Roe v. Wade, Speaks out for the Unborn as She Shares Her New Conviction for Life* (Nashville, TN: Thomas Nelson Publishers, 1997), 231, 195.
9. Burke and Reardon, *Forbidden Grief*, 29.
10. Manning, *The Ragamuffin Gospel*, 98.
11. Malcolm Gladwell, *The Tipping Point: How Little Things Can Make a Difference* (New York, NY: Back Bay Books, 2002), 62-70.
12. Michelle McClain-Walters, *The Ruth Anointing* (Lake Mary, FL: Charisma House, 2018), 32.
13. Jeanette Vought, Post-Abortion Trauma: 9 Steps to Recovery (Grand Rapids, MI: Zondervan, 1991), 103-104.
14. Brennan Manning, *The Wisdom of Tenderness: What Happens When God's Fierce Mercy Transforms Our Lives* (New York, NY: HarperSanFrancisco, 2004), 170.
15. Brown, *The Gifts of Imperfection*, 39.
16. Elliott Institute, *Hope and Healing*, 1998, Volume 6, No. 3, 1-12. https://www.after-abortion.org/hope-and-healing-page-images/
17. Nadia Comanici Quotes, Quotefancy.com, 2023, https://quotefancy.com/quote/1141509/Nadia-Comaneci-I-don-t-run-away-from-a-challenge-because-I-am-afraid-Instead-I-run-toward, accessed September 11, 2023.
18. Ann Brashares Quotes, Quotefancy.com, 2023 ,https://quotefancy.com/quote/19213/Ann-Brashares-You-couldn-t-erase-the-past-You-couldn-t-even-change-it-But-sometimes-life, accessed September 11, 2023.
19. McClain-Walters, *The Ruth Anointing*, 1–2.

8. THE WHISPER

1. Manning, *The Ragamuffin Gospel*, 31.
2. Manning, *The Ragamuffin Gospel*, 32.
3. Weir, *The Truman Show*, 1:26:10-1:26:16.
4. Peterson, *Run with the Horses*, 24–25.

5. Weir, *The Truman Show*, 1:31:48-1:35:15.

6. Lamott, *Bird by Bird* 29-31.

7. Manning, *The Ragamuffin Gospel*, 103.

8. Manning, *The Ragamuffin Gospel*, 77.

9. Frederick Buechner and George Connor, *Listening to Your Life: Daily Meditations with Frederick Buechner* (San Francisco, CA: HarperSanFrancisco, 2007), 236-237.

10. See Isaiah 60:20.

11. Sydna Massé, *Her Choice to Heal: Finding Spiritual and Emotional Peace after Abortion* (Colorado Springs, CO: David C. Cook, 2009), 130.

12. John Sinclair Quotes, Quotefancy.com, 2024, https://quotefancy.com/quote/1652551/John-Sinclair-Failure-is-a-bruise-not-a-tattoo, accessed February 3, 2024.

13. Zig Ziglar Quotes, *See You at the Top (2000)*, Libquotes.com, https://libquotes.com/zig-ziglar/quote/lba0z8g, accessed February 5, 2023.

14. Corrie Ten Boom, Elizabeth Sherrill, and John L. Sherrill, *The Hiding Place* (Grand Rapids, MI: Chosen Books, 2006), 197.

15. McCorvey and Thomas, *Won by Love*, 191.

16. Buechner, *A Crazy, Holy Grace*, 61–62.

17. Manning, *The Ragamuffin Gospel*, 87.

18. Brennan Manning, *The Signature of Jesus: The Call to a Life Marked by Holy Passion and Relentless Faith* (Colorado Springs, CO: Multnomah Books, 1996), 198.

19. Liz Wright and Gretchen Rodriguez, *Loved—A 90 Day Journey Into The Heart Of God* (Liz Wright Ministries, 2021), back cover.

20. Frederick Buechner, *The Magnificent Defeat* (San Francisco, CA: Harper and Row, 1966), 135.

21. Eugene H. Peterson, *Every Step An Arrival: A 90-Day Devotional for Exploring God's Word* (Colorado Springs, CO: WaterBrook, 2018), 35-36.

9. WHITE AS SNOW

1. Kupelian, *The Marketing of Evil*, 211.

2. Hiroo Onoda and Charles S. Terry, *No Surrender My Thirty-Year War* (Annapolis, MD: Naval Institute Press, 2021), 208-219.

3. Madeleine L. Engle, *Walking on Water: Reflections on Faith and Art* (ed. Convergent Books, 2016), https://libquotes.com/madeleine-lengle/quote/lbq7r3t, accessed August 13, 2024.

4. Buechner, *Wishful Thinking*, 38-39.

5. Nicole Nasowski, *What If It's Wonderful? An Invitation to Release Your Fears, Choose Joy, and Find the Courage to Celebrate* (Nashville, TN: W Publishing, 2022), 28.

6. Edward T. Welch, *Shame Interrupted: How God Lifts the Pain of Worthlessness and Rejection* (Greensboro, NC: New Growth Press, 2012), 18.

7. Whole Women's Health. "Message From Our Founder." Accessed August 14, 2024. https://wholewomanshealth.com/message-from-our-founder/.

8. Stephen Covey, *The 7 Habits of Highly Effective People Personal Workbook (ed.*

Simon and Schuster, 2008), https://libquotes.com/stephen-covey/quote/lbd0g5o, Accessed August 13, 2024.

9. George Eliot. AZQuotes.com, Wind and Fly LTD, 2023. https://www.azquotes.com/quote/583127, accessed December 07, 2023.

10. Burke and Reardon, *Forbidden Grief,* 82–83.

11. Bessel A. van der Kolk, M.D., *The Body Keeps the Score: Brain, Mind, and Body in the Healing of Trauma* (New York, NY, Penguin Books: 2014).

12. Buechner, *Wishful Thinking,* 39.

13. See 1 John 1:9 MSG

14. *Vocabulary.com Dictionary,* s.v. "stigma," accessed October 04, 2023, https://www.vocabulary.com/dictionary/stigma.

15. Nathaniel Hawthorne, *The Scarlet Letter* (Mineola, NY: Dover Publications, 1994), 174.

16. Welch, *Shame Interrupted,* 13–14.

17. Harper Douglas, "Etymology of stigma," Online Etymology Dictionary, accessed May 4, 2023, https://www.etymonlinecom/word/stigma

18. *Noah Webster's first edition of an American Dictionary of the English Language:* republished in facsimile edition by the Foundation for American Christian education ..., ed. vols. (2004), s.v. "Stigma.,"

19. Hawthorne, *The Scarlet Letter,* 174.

20. *Noah Webster's first edition of an American Dictionary of the English Language:* republished in facsimile edition by the Foundation for American Christian education ..., ed. vols. (2004), s.v. "Shame.,"

21. Allender and Crabb, The Wounded Heart, 24.

22. Welch, *Shame Interrupted,* 2.

23. Welch, *Shame Interrupted,* 12.

24. Welch, *Shame Interrupted,* 17.

25. Welch, *Shame Interrupted,* 51

26. Albert Schweitzer Quotes. BrainyQuote.com, BrainyMedia Inc, 2023. https://www.brainyquote.com/quotes/albert_schweitzer_402282, accessed October 9, 2023.

27. Buechner, *Wishful Thinking,* 18.

28. Silent No More Awareness Campaign. "What is the Silent No More Awareness Campaign?" Accessed February 23, 2024. https://www.silentnomoreawareness.org/about-us/.

29. See John 8:1-11 NIV.

30. Max Lucado, *He Chose the Nails: What God Did to Win Your Heart* (Nashville, TN: Thomas Nelson, 2000), 17-18.

31. Floyd McClung, *The Father Heart of God: God Loves You, Learn to Know His Compassionate Touch* (Eugene, OR: Harvest House Publishers, 1985), 65-66.

32. Randy Alcorn, *Heaven* (Carol Stream, IL: Tyndale House Publishers, Inc., 2004), 298-299, 355-356.

33. Brennan Manning, *Abba's Child: the Cry of the Heart for Intimate Belonging* (Colorado Springs, CO: NavPress, 2015), 126.

34. Welch, *Shame Interrupted,* 103, 105.

10. FROM GRAVES TO GARDENS

1. Jack London. AZQuotes.com, Wind and Fly LTD, 2024. https://www.azquotes.com/quote/1316511, accessed March 05, 2024.

2. See Romans 8:1 NIV.

3. Ernest Hemingway, *A Farewell to Arms; with an Introd. by Robert Penn Warren* (New York: C. Scribner's Sons, 1929).

4. Buechner, *Wishful Thinking*, 37-38.

5. Buechner, *Wishful Thinking*, 106.

6. Manning, *Abba's Child*, 64.

7. Liz Susong, "Everything You Need to Know About Flower Girls," *Brides*, January 7, 2022. https://www.brides.com/story/where-the-flower-girl-tradition-comes-from

8. Susong, "Everything You Need to Know About Flower Girls"

9. Peterson, *Run with the Horses,* 29-32.

10. Buechner, *Wishful Thinking*, 17.

11. Kathy Gentz, "The Greatest Gift of the Garden," web log, *Https://Washingtongardener.Blogspot.Com* (blog), October 10, 2022, https://washingtongardener.blogspot.com/2022/10/monday-thoughts-greatest-gift-of-garden.html.

12. Phipps, Wintley. "It is Well with My Soul." April 6, 2012. Music video, 1:20-1:46, https://www.youtube.com/watch?v=E8HffdyLd0c&list=PLVtZ_Frat9BCzpyCYe-TemXtU1UoZT0oE4.

13. Kennedy, Amos Paul, Jr., Artist. Where there is no vision, there is no hope. -- George Washington Carver. , 2012. [Alabama: Kennedy Prints] Photograph. https://www.loc.gov/item/2023634982/.

14. See Proverbs 31:25 NASB.

15. See 2 Corinthians 5:21 MSG.

16. Brennan Manning, *The Wisdom of Tenderness: What Happens When God's Fierce Mercy Transforms Our Lives* (New York, NY: HarperSanFrancisco, 2004), 51.

POSTSCRIPT

1. Beuchner, *A Crazy Holy Grace*, 130.

2. Nathanson, *The Hand of God*, 195.